HOW TO

SELL AMAZON

RETURN PALLETS

TURNING LIQUIDATION INTO CASH

CARTER BLAKE

CONTENTS

INTRODUCTION

Imagine transforming a seemingly mundane task into a profitable venture that not only fills your pockets but also offers a sense of accomplishment and entrepreneurial satisfaction. Welcome to the world of buying and selling Amazon return pallets, a niche yet burgeoning market that has captured the attention of savvy entrepreneurs and side-hustlers alike. This book is your comprehensive guide to navigating this unique landscape, turning liquidation into cash with strategic know-how and insightful tips.

The allure of Amazon return pallets lies in their potential. Each pallet is a treasure trove of returned items, overstock, and unsold inventory from the world's largest online retailer. These pallets can include anything from electronics and household goods to clothing and toys, offering a diverse array of products that can be resold for profit. However, the key to success in this venture isn't merely purchasing these pallets; it involves a keen understanding of the market, strategic buying decisions, effective selling techniques, and an organized approach to inventory management.

Throughout the pages of this book, you will uncover the intricacies of sourcing Amazon return pallets, identifying the most profitable categories, and negotiating the best deals. We will delve into the various platforms and auction sites where these pallets are sold, providing you with tips on how to discern reputable sellers from those less trustworthy. The book also covers essential aspects of logistics, including shipping considerations, storage solutions, and the tools you'll need to efficiently process and list your items for resale.

Moreover, we will explore the art of resale across different platforms, from eBay and Craigslist to specialized online marketplaces and even local sales channels. You will learn how to create compelling product listings, set competitive prices, and manage customer interactions to build a positive reputation and ensure repeat business. Case studies and real-life examples will illustrate the successes and pitfalls of others in this field, offering valuable lessons and inspiration.

Whether you are a seasoned entrepreneur looking to diversify your income streams or a beginner eager to dip your toes into the world of reselling, this book provides the knowledge and tools you need to turn Amazon return pallets into a lucrative and sustainable business.

Chapter 1: Introduction to Amazon Return Pallets

UNDERSTANDING RETURN PALLETS

Return pallets represent an intriguing facet of the retail world, especially when it comes to Amazon. These pallets consist of items that customers have returned to Amazon for various reasons. Some products may be in perfect condition, while others could have minor defects, damaged packaging, or be completely non-functional. Understanding the intricacies of these return pallets is crucial for anyone looking to profit from buying and selling them.

The first thing to note is the diversity of items you can find in a return pallet. From electronics and household goods to clothing and toys, the range is vast. This diversity is both an opportunity and a challenge. On one hand, it means that there is potential for high-value items to be included, offering significant profit margins. On the other hand, it requires a keen eye for detail and an understanding of various product categories to accurately assess the value of the pallet.

Condition is a key factor when dealing with return pallets. Items are usually categorized based on their state, such as "like new," "open box," "used," or "for parts or not working." This categorization helps in estimating the resale value. "Like new" items are typically the most desirable, as they can be sold at a higher price with minimal effort. "Open box" items might have been used briefly or just have damaged packaging but are generally in good working condition. "Used" items can vary widely in terms of wear and tear, and "for parts or not working" items are often sold to individuals who can repair or repurpose them.

The source of return pallets also matters. Amazon offers these pallets through various liquidation platforms and auction sites. Each platform has its own set of rules, fees, and quality assurances, which can affect the overall profitability. Some platforms provide detailed manifests of the pallet contents, while others may offer only a general overview. Detailed manifests are invaluable as they allow for a more accurate assessment of potential profit and risk.

Pricing strategies for return pallets can also vary. Some pallets are sold at a flat rate, while others are auctioned off to the highest bidder. Understanding the pricing dynamics of each platform is essential. It's not just about the initial cost of the pallet; shipping fees, handling costs, and potential refurbishment expenses must all be factored into the total investment. The goal is to ensure that the resale value of the items exceeds these combined costs.

Risk management is another critical aspect. Not every pallet will be profitable, and some may even result in a loss. It's important to start with a budget that you can afford to lose and to diversify your purchases to spread out the risk. Building relationships with reliable suppliers and gaining experience over time will help mitigate some of these risks.

In essence, return pallets offer a unique opportunity for entrepreneurs willing to navigate their complexities. From understanding the condition and diversity of items to mastering the intricacies of various liquidation platforms, a comprehensive approach is necessary. The potential for high rewards exists, but it comes with its set of challenges that require careful consideration and strategy.

THE RESALE MARKET

The resale market is essentially a second-chance marketplace where returned, overstocked, or slightly damaged goods find new homes. Understanding its intricacies is crucial for anyone looking to capitalize on the potential profits hidden within these return pallets.

The resale market thrives on the principle of value recovery. Retailers, eager to recoup some of their investment from returned items, liquidate these goods at significantly reduced prices. These items, ranging from electronics and apparel to home goods and toys, often end up in the hands of resellers who see the potential for profit. The key to success lies in discerning the quality and demand of these products, ensuring they meet the expectations of secondary buyers.

One of the most intriguing aspects of the resale market is its unpredictability. Each pallet is a mystery, filled with items that can vary greatly in condition and desirability. This uncertainty is part of the allure, offering the thrill of discovery with each purchase. For resellers, this means honing skills in evaluation and risk management. The ability to quickly assess the potential resale value of items and make informed purchasing decisions is invaluable.

The resale market also demands a keen understanding of customer preferences and market trends. Successful resellers stay attuned to what consumers are currently seeking, adapting their inventory to match these demands. This requires continuous market research and a flexible approach, as trends can shift rapidly. Building a diverse inventory that appeals to a broad audience can mitigate the risks associated with fluctuating consumer interests.

Effective marketing strategies play a pivotal role in the resale market. Resellers must be adept at creating compelling listings that highlight the value and appeal of their products. High-quality photographs, detailed descriptions, and transparent information about the condition of items are essential components of successful listings. Leveraging various online platforms, from dedicated resale websites to social media channels, can significantly enhance visibility and reach a wider audience.

The resale market is not without its challenges. Competition can be fierce, with many resellers vying for the same customer base. Establishing a reputation for reliability and quality is crucial. This involves not only offering good products but also providing excellent customer service. Prompt communication, fair pricing, and hassle-free returns can build trust and encourage repeat business.

Networking with other resellers and industry professionals can provide valuable insights and support. Sharing experiences and strategies can lead to new opportunities and collaborations. Attending trade shows, participating in online forums, and joining reseller groups can expand one's knowledge and connections within the industry.

The resale market is a dynamic and ever-evolving landscape, offering endless possibilities for those willing to navigate its complexities. With the right approach, resellers can turn Amazon return pallets into profitable ventures, transforming what might seem like a gamble into a calculated and rewarding enterprise.

BENEFITS OF BUYING RETURN PALLETS

The allure of buying Amazon return pallets often lies in the potential for substantial profits and the thrill of discovering hidden treasures within each shipment. These pallets, bursting with a variety of returned items, offer a unique opportunity for both seasoned resellers and newcomers to the world of e-commerce. The benefits of purchasing these pallets extend beyond mere financial gain, encompassing aspects such as sustainability, variety, and the sheer excitement of the unknown.

One of the primary advantages is the potential for significant profit margins. Return pallets are typically sold at a fraction of the retail price, allowing buyers to acquire a large volume of goods for a relatively low investment. This cost-efficiency is particularly appealing for small business owners and individual resellers who are looking to maximize their return on investment. By carefully inspecting and testing the items, savvy buyers can identify products that are in excellent condition or require minimal refurbishment, thereby increasing their resale value.

Another notable benefit is the sheer diversity of items that can be found within a single pallet. These pallets often contain an eclectic mix of products, ranging from electronics and home goods to clothing and toys. This variety not only enhances the excitement of unboxing but also broadens the potential customer base for resellers. By offering a wide range of products, sellers can attract different demographics and meet varying consumer needs, thereby enhancing their market reach and sales potential.

The element of surprise associated with return pallets adds an exhilarating dimension to the buying process. Each pallet is a mystery waiting to be unraveled, and the anticipation of uncovering valuable or rare items can be immensely satisfying. This thrill of discovery can make the process of buying and reselling return pallets more engaging and enjoyable, transforming it from a mere business transaction into an adventurous pursuit.

Sustainability is another compelling reason to consider purchasing return pallets. In an era where environmental consciousness is increasingly important, buying and reselling returned goods helps reduce waste. Many items that are returned to retailers are still in good condition but cannot be resold at full price due to damaged packaging or minor defects. By purchasing these items, resellers are effectively giving them a second life, thereby contributing to a more sustainable and circular economy.

Moreover, the process of handling return pallets can be educational and enriching. For those new to the reselling business, it offers a hands-on learning experience that encompasses various aspects of e-commerce, from product evaluation and pricing to marketing and customer service. This practical knowledge is invaluable and can serve as a strong foundation for building a successful reselling enterprise.

Networking opportunities also arise from participating in the return pallet market. Buyers often connect with other resellers, wholesalers, and industry professionals, creating a supportive community where knowledge and resources are shared. These connections can lead to collaborative ventures, bulk purchasing deals, and valuable insights that can enhance one's business acumen and operational efficiency.

In essence, the benefits of buying Amazon return pallets are multifaceted, offering financial rewards, diverse product offerings, excitement, sustainability, educational value, and networking opportunities. This multifaceted approach not only makes the venture profitable but also enriching and fulfilling, appealing to a wide array of individuals and businesses looking to thrive in the dynamic world of e-commerce.

POTENTIAL CHALLENGES

Engaging in the business of buying and selling Amazon return pallets can be an exciting and potentially lucrative venture. However, it is not without its challenges. One of the foremost difficulties is the unpredictability of the contents within each pallet. Despite any manifest or inventory list provided, there is no absolute guarantee that all items will be in working condition or even present. This uncertainty requires a keen eye for detail and a willingness to accept that not every purchase will yield high-value items.

Another significant challenge is the condition of the returned items. Amazon return pallets often contain a mix of new, used, and defective products. While some items may be in pristine condition, others could be damaged or missing parts. It is essential to have a systematic approach to inspecting, testing, and refurbishing these items. Investing time and resources into repairs and quality checks is necessary to ensure that the products you sell meet customer expectations.

Storage and logistics present additional hurdles. Handling large quantities of goods requires ample storage space, which can be costly. Efficiently organizing and managing inventory is crucial to avoid losses and ensure smooth operations. Furthermore, shipping these items to customers involves careful packaging and an understanding of shipping regulations and costs. Mishandling these aspects can lead to increased expenses and customer dissatisfaction.

Market competition is another challenge not to be underestimated. The popularity of buying and selling return pallets has grown, leading to a more crowded marketplace. Standing out in such a competitive environment demands strategic planning, effective marketing, and exceptional customer service. Building a reputable brand that customers trust is key to gaining a competitive edge.

Financial risks are inherent in this business model. The initial investment in purchasing pallets can be substantial, and there is no guarantee of immediate profit. It is vital to have a clear budget and financial plan in place. This includes accounting for potential losses, unexpected expenses, and the time it may take to see a return on investment. Diversifying the types of pallets purchased and having multiple revenue streams can help mitigate these risks.

Navigating legal and regulatory requirements is another critical aspect. Understanding consumer protection laws, return policies, and warranty obligations is necessary to avoid legal complications. Compliance with these regulations ensures that your business operates ethically and transparently. It is also important to stay informed about changes in laws that may impact your business.

Lastly, customer satisfaction plays a pivotal role in the success of selling Amazon return pallets. Handling returns, addressing complaints, and providing excellent customer service are integral to maintaining a positive reputation. Negative reviews or poor customer experiences can significantly impact your business. Developing a robust customer service strategy and ensuring that your team is well-trained in handling various customer scenarios is essential.

In summary, while the business of buying and selling Amazon return pallets offers numerous opportunities, it also comes with its set of challenges. These include the unpredictability of pallet contents, the condition of returned items, storage and logistics issues, market competition, financial risks, legal and regulatory requirements, and the necessity of maintaining high customer satisfaction. Addressing these challenges with careful planning, strategic thinking, and a commitment to quality and customer service can pave the way for a successful and sustainable business.

Chapter 2: Getting Started with Return Pallets

SETTING UP YOUR BUSINESS

The first rays of dawn filter through the window, casting a warm glow on the desktop scattered with notes, business plans, and a steaming cup of coffee. The room is filled with the hum of anticipation, a sense of purpose that signifies the beginning of a new venture. The foundation of your business begins here, in this moment of quiet preparation.

Imagine a space dedicated to your entrepreneurial dreams, a corner where creativity and strategy converge. It's essential to designate a workspace that fosters productivity and focus. Whether it's a home office, a garage, or a rented warehouse, this space will be the nucleus of your operations. Ensure it's organized, well-lit, and equipped with the necessary tools – a computer, reliable internet connection, and ample storage for inventory.

The next step is to formalize your business structure. This involves deciding whether to operate as a sole proprietorship, partnership, limited liability company (LLC), or corporation. Each structure has its own implications for liability, taxes, and paperwork. A sole proprietorship offers simplicity and control, yet it also means personal liability for business debts. An LLC, on the other hand, provides a shield for personal assets while offering flexibility in management and tax benefits. Consulting with a legal advisor can provide clarity and help navigate these choices.

With the structure in place, it's time to register your business. This process varies by location but generally involves selecting a unique business name, filing the necessary paperwork with state and local governments, and obtaining an Employer Identification Number (EIN) from the IRS. This number is crucial for tax purposes and for opening a business bank account.

A business bank account separates personal and business finances, simplifying accounting and offering a professional image to suppliers and customers. Many banks offer specialized accounts with benefits tailored to small businesses, such as lower fees and business credit cards. Establishing a relationship with a bank early on can also be beneficial for future financing needs.

Insurance is another critical aspect. It safeguards your business against unforeseen events such as theft, damage, or legal claims. General liability insurance is a good starting point, covering basic risks associated with running a business. Depending on the scale and nature of your operations, you might also consider additional coverage like property insurance, product liability insurance, or business interruption insurance.

To navigate the world of Amazon return pallets effectively, understanding the market is key. Research where to source these pallets, which suppliers offer the best deals, and what types of products typically yield the highest returns. Websites like Direct Liquidation, BULQ, and Liquidation.com are popular starting points. Building relationships with reliable suppliers can provide access to better deals and more consistent inventory.

Creating an online presence is vital. A professional website serves as your digital storefront, showcasing your products and establishing credibility. Investing time in learning about search engine optimization (SEO) can drive traffic to your site. Social media platforms also offer powerful tools for marketing and customer engagement. Regular updates, engaging content, and responsive customer service can build a loyal customer base.

As the pieces fall into place, the vision of your business starts to take shape. The journey from an idea to a tangible enterprise is paved with meticulous planning and strategic decisions, setting the stage for a successful venture in the dynamic world of Amazon return pallets.

LEGAL CONSIDERATIONS

The first aspect to consider is the legality of purchasing and reselling returned goods. In most jurisdictions, it is perfectly legal to buy and sell returned items, but it is crucial to familiarize oneself with local laws that may govern these transactions. This involves understanding consumer protection laws, resale regulations, and any specific stipulations that might apply to liquidated goods.

One important legal consideration is obtaining the proper licenses and permits. Depending on your location and the scale of your operations, you might need a resale license or a business permit. These licenses are typically issued by local or state authorities and are essential for legally operating a resale business. They also enable you to purchase goods without paying sales tax, which can significantly impact your profit margins.

Another critical area to explore is the issue of warranties and guarantees. When dealing with Amazon return pallets, it's important to recognize that these items are often sold "as-is," meaning they come with no warranty or guarantee from Amazon. This can affect your business in two ways. First, you must be transparent with your customers about the condition of the items you are selling. Clear communication regarding the lack of warranties can help manage customer expectations and reduce the risk of disputes.

Second, you need to consider your own policies on returns and refunds. While Amazon might not offer a warranty, you can choose to provide some form of guarantee to your customers to build trust and encourage repeat business. However, offering such guarantees also comes with legal obligations, so it's wise to consult with a legal expert to draft clear and fair terms and conditions that protect both your business and your customers.

Intellectual property rights are another significant legal aspect to be aware of. Some returned items may include branded products, and reselling these can sometimes lead to trademark or copyright issues. It is essential to verify that the products you are reselling do not infringe on any intellectual property rights. This might involve checking for counterfeit goods and ensuring that all branded items are genuine. Selling counterfeit items can lead to severe legal consequences, including hefty fines and even criminal charges.

Data protection and privacy laws also come into play, especially if you are collecting customer information. Compliance with regulations such as the General Data Protection Regulation (GDPR) in Europe or the California Consumer Privacy Act (CCPA) in the United States is vital. These laws dictate how you must handle, store, and protect customer data. Failure to comply can result in significant penalties and damage to your business's reputation.

Insurance is another practical consideration. Having the right insurance can protect your business from various risks, including liability claims, property damage, and theft. Business liability insurance, in particular, can safeguard you against claims related to the products you sell. Consulting with an insurance agent to tailor a policy that fits your specific needs is a prudent step.

Understanding and adhering to these legal considerations not only helps in running a compliant and ethical business but also builds a foundation of trust with your customers and partners. By taking the time to address these legal aspects, you can focus on maximizing the potential of your Amazon return pallet business while minimizing the risks.

INITIAL INVESTMENT

Venturing into the world of buying and selling Amazon return pallets requires a keen understanding of the initial investment involved. The first step is to recognize the financial commitment necessary to get started. This includes not only the cost of the pallets themselves but also additional expenditures that may arise along the way.

The price of Amazon return pallets can vary significantly depending on several factors. These factors include the type of products contained within the pallets, the condition of the items, and the supplier's pricing strategy. Some pallets might contain high-value electronics, while others might be filled with household goods or clothing. The diversity in product type necessitates a thorough analysis before purchase. A savvy investor will spend time researching different suppliers and comparing prices to ensure they are getting the best deal possible.

Beyond the cost of the pallets, there are other essential financial considerations. Shipping fees can add a substantial amount to the initial investment. The weight and size of the pallets, as well as the distance they need to be transported, will influence shipping costs. It is crucial to factor these expenses into the budget to avoid any unexpected financial strain.

Storage is another critical aspect of the initial investment. Once the pallets are purchased and shipped, they need to be stored in a safe and organized manner. Renting a storage unit or utilizing a section of one's home or business premises are potential solutions. The cost of storage will depend on the size and location of the space. Ensuring that the storage area is secure and adequately protected from environmental factors is vital to preserving the integrity of the products.

Investing in basic equipment and tools is also necessary to facilitate the sorting and processing of items within the pallets. This might include shelving units, tables, boxes, and packing materials. Having the right tools on hand will streamline the process and enhance efficiency, ultimately saving time and money.

Another important consideration is the potential need for labor. Depending on the volume of pallets being handled, it might be necessary to hire additional help. This could range from part-time assistants to full-time employees. The cost of labor should be calculated and included in the initial investment plan.

Insurance is an often-overlooked expense but an essential part of the investment. Protecting the inventory from potential risks such as theft, damage, or loss is crucial. Various insurance options are available, and selecting the right coverage will provide peace of mind and financial security.

Marketing and sales strategies also require an initial investment. Creating an online presence, whether through a dedicated website or through platforms like eBay, Amazon, or social media, involves costs. These costs include website hosting fees, professional photography for product listings, and possibly advertising expenses. Effective marketing will play a significant role in the success of selling the items from the return pallets.

Lastly, it is wise to set aside a contingency fund. This fund will act as a financial buffer for any unforeseen expenses that may arise during the initial stages of the business. Having a contingency fund ensures that the venture can continue smoothly without being derailed by unexpected costs.

Understanding and planning for these various financial aspects will lay a solid foundation for success. Careful budgeting and prudent financial management are essential to navigating the initial investment phase and paving the way for a profitable business in the world of Amazon return pallets.

FINDING RELIABLE SOURCES

In the quest to master the art of buying and selling Amazon return pallets, one of the most crucial steps lies in identifying reliable sources. Imagine navigating a vast marketplace brimming with potential, yet also fraught with the risk of encountering disreputable vendors. The key to success in this endeavor is to meticulously discern which sources are trustworthy.

Begin by delving into the online realm, where numerous platforms offer Amazon return pallets. Websites dedicated to liquidation and wholesale merchandise serve as the primary hunting ground for these hidden treasures. However, not all platforms are created equal. It is essential to conduct thorough research on each website's reputation. Look for reviews and testimonials from previous buyers. These candid accounts provide valuable insights into the authenticity and reliability of the source.

Another critical aspect is verifying the legitimacy of the vendors. Many websites feature multiple sellers, and it is paramount to ensure that the individual or company you are dealing with has a solid track record. Investigate their history, the quality of the merchandise they offer, and their customer service standards. A reputable vendor will have a history of satisfied customers and a transparent return policy, which can be a safety net in case the pallets do not meet your expectations.

Networking within the industry can also be an invaluable tool in finding reliable sources. Engaging with other resellers through forums, social media groups, and industry events can lead to recommendations for trustworthy vendors. These connections can provide first-hand accounts of experiences with different sources, helping to steer you toward reputable sellers and away from those who might not deliver as promised.

Pay attention to the details provided in the listings. Reliable sources will offer comprehensive descriptions of the pallets, including the condition of the items, any potential defects, and the overall value. Transparency in these descriptions is a hallmark of a trustworthy seller. They should also provide clear and accurate photographs of the items included in the pallet. This visual representation allows you to better assess the potential value and quality of the merchandise.

It is also wise to consider the payment methods accepted by the vendor. Secure payment options such as credit cards or escrow services can offer an additional layer of protection. Avoid vendors who insist on unconventional payment methods, as this can be a red flag for potential scams.

Customer service is another critical indicator of a reliable source. Vendors who are responsive and willing to answer your questions demonstrate a commitment to customer satisfaction. They should be able to provide detailed information about the pallets, shipping processes, and any other concerns you may have. A vendor who values communication and transparency is more likely to be a reliable partner in your reselling journey.

Lastly, be mindful of the pricing. While it can be tempting to go for the lowest price available, it is important to balance cost with quality and reliability. Sometimes, an offer that seems too good to be true might be just that. A slightly higher investment in a reputable source can pay off in the long run through higher quality merchandise and fewer headaches.

In the intricate world of buying and selling Amazon return pallets, finding reliable sources is the cornerstone of success. By conducting diligent research, networking within the community, and prioritizing transparency and customer service, you can navigate this complex landscape with confidence and savvy.

Chapter 3: Sourcing High-Value Pallets

IDENTIFYING HIGH-VALUE ITEMS

Walking through the vast, often overwhelming world of Amazon return pallets, one must possess the keen eye of a seasoned treasure hunter. These pallets, stacked high and filled with an eclectic mix of items, hold the potential for remarkable finds. The key lies in discerning which items are not just valuable, but highly sought after in the resale market. This skill, though seemingly daunting at first, can be honed with practice and a bit of insider knowledge.

The first step in this process is understanding the types of items that generally hold higher value. Electronics, for instance, are often a goldmine. From smartphones and tablets to gaming consoles and smart home devices, these items typically retain a significant portion of their retail value even when returned. However, it's crucial to inspect these items thoroughly for functionality and completeness. Missing accessories or minor cosmetic damages can drastically affect their resale value.

Another category to keep an eye on is branded clothing and accessories. High-end fashion items, especially those from well-known designers, can fetch a good price on the secondary market. When examining clothing, look for tags, original packaging, and any signs of wear or damage. Shoes, handbags, and watches from renowned brands are also highly desirable. Authenticity is paramount in this category, so familiarizing oneself with the hallmarks of genuine products is essential.

Home and kitchen appliances are another promising area. Items like coffee makers, blenders, vacuum cleaners, and air purifiers are often returned in near-new condition. These items are not only practical but also in constant demand. Before deciding to resell, ensure they are in working order and come with all necessary parts and manuals.

Toys and baby products can also be surprisingly lucrative. High-quality toys, especially those from popular brands or those that are educational, tend to sell well. Baby gear, such as strollers, car seats, and baby monitors, are often returned simply because the child outgrew them or the parents changed their minds. These items must meet safety standards and be in excellent condition to attract buyers.

Books, although often overlooked, can be a hidden gem. First editions, signed copies, and rare finds can be particularly valuable. Additionally, textbooks and popular series have a steady market. Condition is vital here; books should be free from significant damage, markings, or missing pages.

Specialty items, such as fitness equipment, outdoor gear, and musical instruments, can also yield high returns. These items cater to niche markets but often come with a higher price tag. Ensuring they are in prime condition and understanding their specific market demand can lead to profitable sales.

Knowledge of current market trends is invaluable. Keeping an eye on what's trending, seasonality, and consumer demand can guide your buying decisions. Online platforms and resale sites can provide insights into what items are selling fast and at what prices.

Ultimately, patience and a willingness to research are your best allies. Not every pallet will contain high-value items, and it may take time to develop a discerning eye. Carefully evaluate each item for its condition, market demand, and potential resale value. Over time, this practice will become second nature, and the ability to identify high-value items will significantly enhance your success in buying and selling Amazon return pallets.

ONLINE MARKETPLACES

Online marketplaces can be both exhilarating and daunting, especially for those looking to buy and sell Amazon return pallets. These digital platforms serve as bustling bazaars where sellers and buyers converge, each with their unique items and aspirations. The key to success lies in understanding the landscape, identifying trustworthy platforms, and mastering the art of negotiation.

The first step in this digital journey involves selecting the right marketplace. Websites like eBay, Liquidation.com, and Direct Liquidation have become popular hubs for Amazon return pallets. Each platform has its own set of rules, fees, and user interfaces. eBay, known for its auction-style listings, allows sellers to reach a global audience. Liquidation.com, on the other hand, specializes in bulk sales, making it a go-to for those looking to purchase pallets in large quantities. Direct Liquidation offers a more straightforward approach with fixed prices and detailed item descriptions.

Trust is paramount in online transactions. Reviews and ratings provide valuable insights into the credibility of sellers. A high rating coupled with positive feedback from previous buyers can be a good indicator of reliability. However, it's essential to read between the lines. Sometimes, even highly-rated sellers may have occasional negative reviews. Analyzing these reviews can help in understanding common issues and how the seller addresses them.

The art of negotiation plays a crucial role in securing the best deals. While some platforms offer fixed prices, others allow for price negotiations. Understanding the market value of the items within the pallets can provide leverage during these discussions. It's beneficial to remain polite yet firm, ensuring that both parties feel satisfied with the transaction. Building a rapport with sellers can also lead to better deals in the future, as trust and mutual respect grow.

Detailed research is the cornerstone of successful buying and selling. Before purchasing a pallet, it's crucial to know what it contains. Some marketplaces provide detailed manifests listing the items, their conditions, and estimated retail values. This transparency allows buyers to make informed decisions and assess potential profits. Conversely, when selling, providing clear and honest descriptions can attract serious buyers and reduce the likelihood of disputes.

Shipping and logistics are another critical aspect to consider. The size and weight of return pallets often mean higher shipping costs. Some online marketplaces offer shipping services or partnerships with logistics companies, simplifying the process. However, understanding these costs upfront and factoring them into the overall budget is essential. For sellers, offering flexible shipping options can attract more buyers and expedite sales.

Customer service and support from the marketplace can significantly impact the buying and selling experience. Platforms with robust support systems can assist in resolving disputes, navigating issues, and providing guidance. Familiarizing oneself with the marketplace's policies regarding returns, disputes, and seller protection can prevent potential pitfalls.

The digital nature of these marketplaces also means staying updated with the latest trends and changes. Regularly visiting forums, attending webinars, and networking with other buyers and sellers can provide valuable insights and tips. This continuous learning process ensures staying ahead of the competition and adapting to the ever-evolving online marketplace landscape.

By mastering these aspects, one can effectively navigate the complex yet rewarding world of online marketplaces, turning Amazon return pallets into profitable ventures.

AUCTION SITES

Auction sites offer a dynamic avenue for acquiring Amazon return pallets, presenting an environment that pulses with the excitement of bidding wars and the allure of potential treasure troves. These platforms serve as bustling marketplaces where sellers list return pallets, and buyers compete to secure them, often at prices significantly lower than retail value. The very nature of auction sites injects a sense of urgency and competition, making the experience both exhilarating and potentially rewarding.

Upon entering the digital realm of auction sites, one is immediately struck by the sheer variety of listings. Each pallet is often accompanied by detailed descriptions, photographs, and sometimes even manifest lists that provide insights into the contents. This transparency can be a double-edged sword; while it allows buyers to make informed decisions, it also attracts more bidders, potentially driving up the final price. Seasoned buyers often develop a keen eye for spotting undervalued pallets and can quickly assess the potential profitability of a lot.

Navigating auction sites requires a blend of strategy, patience, and a bit of luck. Successful bidders often employ a systematic approach, setting clear budgets and sticking to them. It's easy to get caught up in the heat of the moment and overbid, so disciplined bidding is crucial. Many platforms offer features like automatic bidding, where buyers can set their maximum bid and let the system incrementally increase their offer as needed. This can be a useful tool to prevent emotional overspending and to ensure that bids remain within budgetary constraints.

Auction sites also vary in terms of the type of return pallets they offer. Some specialize in specific categories such as electronics, apparel, or home goods, while others provide a more general selection. Understanding the niche or focus of a particular site can help buyers target their efforts more effectively. For instance, a buyer interested in high-end electronics might frequent a site known for tech-heavy pallets, whereas someone looking for a diverse mix of household items might prefer a more generalized platform.

The competitive nature of auction sites means that timing can be everything. Auctions are often time-bound, with listings available for a limited period. Savvy buyers keep a close watch on the closing times of auctions, sometimes swooping in with strategic bids in the final moments to secure a pallet. This tactic, known as "sniping," can be highly effective but also comes with its risks, as other bidders may have the same idea.

In addition to the competitive aspect, auction sites often foster a sense of community among buyers. Forums, comment sections, and review systems allow users to share their experiences, offer advice, and even warn others about potential pitfalls. Engaging with these communities can provide valuable insights and help buyers refine their strategies. Networking with other users can also lead to collaborations, such as group buys or shared shipping costs, further enhancing the overall buying experience.

The thrill of winning an auction, combined with the anticipation of uncovering the contents of a return pallet, makes auction sites a compelling option for both novice and experienced buyers. The key to success lies in thorough research, disciplined bidding, and strategic timing. With these elements in place, auction sites can serve as a fruitful source of Amazon return pallets, offering both the excitement of the chase and the potential for significant financial gain.

DIRECT FROM AMAZON

One of the most straightforward and reliable methods to acquire these return pallets is directly from Amazon itself. This approach offers a level of convenience and assurance that can be incredibly appealing to both novice and seasoned buyers.

Amazon's liquidation program is designed to manage the vast quantities of returned items that accumulate daily. These returns can range from high-end electronics to everyday household items, providing a diverse array of products for potential resale. By purchasing directly from Amazon, buyers can often access higher-quality goods compared to other sources, as the company maintains strict standards for the products it sells.

The first step in purchasing Amazon return pallets directly is to understand the various platforms and programs Amazon offers. One of the primary avenues is through Amazon's Liquidation Auctions, a platform where Amazon sells off its excess and returned inventory. Here, buyers can bid on pallets in an auction-style format, often securing goods at a fraction of their original cost. This platform requires registration and approval, ensuring that only serious buyers participate.

Another option is Amazon's Warehouse Deals, which offers discounted prices on returned, warehouse-damaged, used, or refurbished products. While this platform is more retail-oriented, it still provides an excellent opportunity for buyers to acquire individual items at reduced prices, which can then be bundled and sold as part of a larger pallet.

Understanding the grading system used by Amazon is crucial when purchasing return pallets. Items are typically categorized based on their condition, ranging from new or like-new to used or for parts only. This grading system helps buyers assess the potential resale value of the items within a pallet. For instance, a pallet with a majority of like-new items will likely yield higher returns compared to one filled with items marked for parts.

The bidding process on Amazon's Liquidation Auctions can be competitive, requiring strategic planning and a keen eye for value. Prospective buyers should thoroughly research past auction results and current market trends to make informed bids. Setting a budget and sticking to it is essential to avoid overpaying for a pallet. Additionally, understanding the shipping costs associated with these pallets is vital, as they can significantly impact the overall profitability.

Once a pallet is secured, the next step is to inspect and sort the items. This process involves evaluating each item's condition, functionality, and market value. Proper documentation and organization are key to efficiently managing and reselling the goods. Utilizing online marketplaces such as eBay, Craigslist, or even Amazon itself can help reach a broader audience and maximize profits.

Building a relationship with Amazon's liquidation team can also be advantageous. Regular buyers who demonstrate reliability and volume purchases may receive preferential treatment, such as early access to new pallets or exclusive deals. Networking within this niche market can lead to valuable insights and opportunities, enhancing the overall buying and selling experience.

Purchasing Amazon return pallets directly from the source offers a blend of reliability, quality, and potential profitability. With careful research, strategic bidding, and effective resale tactics, buyers can turn Amazon's returned goods into a thriving business venture.

Chapter 4: Evaluating Return Pallets

INSPECTING PALLETS

When evaluating Amazon return pallets, the first and perhaps most crucial step is a thorough inspection. Each pallet tells a story through its contents, and deciphering this narrative requires a keen eye and a patient approach. The process begins by examining the exterior. The condition of the wrapping and the pallet itself can provide initial insights into how the items were handled and stored. A tightly wrapped pallet with no visible damage suggests care in packaging and transport, while torn or loose wrapping may indicate rough handling.

As the wrapping is removed, the true nature of the pallet's contents begins to reveal itself. This moment is akin to peeling back the layers of an onion, where each layer holds potential surprises. One must be prepared for a diverse range of items, from electronics to household goods, each with varying degrees of wear and tear. The key is to methodically sort through each item, assessing its condition and potential resale value.

A systematic approach is essential. Starting from the top and working downwards ensures that no item is overlooked. Each product should be inspected for signs of damage, such as scratches, dents, or missing parts. Electronics, for example, should be checked for functionality. Plugging them in and powering them on can quickly determine whether they are in working order. For items that require batteries, bringing a set of standard batteries can be incredibly useful.

The packaging of each item also provides valuable information. Original packaging often indicates a higher likelihood that the item is either new or barely used. Conversely, items without packaging or with damaged packaging might have been returned due to defects or dissatisfaction. It's essential to document these observations meticulously, noting the condition and any potential issues.

Another critical aspect of inspecting pallets is identifying any high-value items. These gems can significantly impact the overall profitability of the pallet. High-value items often come with serial numbers or model numbers, which can be cross-referenced online to ascertain their market value. Smartphones, tablets, and other electronics typically fall into this category and should be given extra attention during the inspection.

Equally important is the identification of any items that may pose risks, such as recalled products or those with safety concerns.

Researching the items online can provide information on any recalls or common issues associated with specific products. Safety should always be a priority, and any item that poses a potential hazard should be handled with caution.

As the inspection progresses, it's beneficial to categorize the items based on their condition and potential resale value. Creating separate piles for new, like-new, used, and damaged items helps in organizing and planning the next steps. This categorization also aids in determining the overall worth of the pallet and strategizing the most effective way to sell the items.

The final part of the inspection involves a comprehensive review of the findings. Summarizing the condition of the pallet's contents, the potential resale value, and any identified risks provides a clear picture of the pallet's worth. This detailed assessment is invaluable for making informed decisions about purchasing and selling Amazon return pallets. Through careful inspection and documentation, one can uncover hidden treasures and ensure a profitable venture in the world of Amazon return pallets.

ASSESSING ITEM CONDITIONS

When diving into the world of Amazon return pallets, understanding the condition of the items is paramount. Each pallet is a treasure trove of potential, but discerning the quality of these treasures requires a keen eye and a strategic approach. The first step in this process is familiarizing oneself with the different categories of item conditions. Amazon typically classifies returned items into several conditions: new, like new, very good, good, acceptable, and uninspected returns. Each category offers insights into what you might expect when unboxing your pallet.

New items are pristine, often in their original packaging, and have never been used. These items are the gems of any return pallet, offering the highest resale value with minimal effort. Like new items are nearly flawless, possibly opened but unused, and usually retain their original packaging. These items require a bit more scrutiny, but they often prove to be just as valuable as new items.

Very good items show minor signs of use but are generally in excellent working condition. They might have small cosmetic imperfections or damaged packaging, but their functionality remains uncompromised. Good items have more noticeable wear and tear. They might have been used more extensively, and while they still function properly, they may require a bit more effort to prepare for resale. Acceptable items are the most heavily used and may have significant cosmetic damage or missing parts. These items may require repair or might only be suitable for parts.

Uninspected returns are the wild cards. These items have not been checked for condition, so they can range from brand new to non-functional. This category presents the highest risk but can also yield the highest rewards for those willing to invest the time and effort into sorting and assessing each item.

Once you have a grasp of these categories, the next step is to physically inspect the items. Start by examining the packaging. Original, intact packaging often indicates a higher likelihood that the item is in good condition. However, don't be discouraged by damaged or missing packaging—many items inside could still be in excellent shape.

Carefully unbox each item and conduct a thorough visual inspection. Look for obvious signs of wear, such as scratches, dents, or missing components. If the item is electronic, check for any visible damage to cords, screens, or connectors. For clothing or textiles, inspect for stains, tears, or signs of wear.

Functionality is another critical aspect. For electronics, plug them in and test their basic functions. For mechanical items, ensure all moving parts operate smoothly. This step not only helps you determine the item's condition but also provides peace of mind to potential buyers.

Documentation plays a crucial role in this process. Keep detailed records of each item's condition, including photographs and notes on any defects or issues. This documentation will be invaluable when listing items for resale, as it allows you to provide accurate descriptions and set appropriate prices.

Understanding and assessing item conditions is both an art and a science. It requires a blend of knowledge, attention to detail, and a bit of intuition. By mastering this skill, you can maximize the value of your Amazon return pallets and build a reputation for selling quality items. Each pallet is a new opportunity, and with careful assessment, you can turn these opportunities into profitable ventures.

ESTIMATING RESALE VALUE

The ability to accurately estimate the resale value of items can be the backbone of a successful venture. Each pallet, a treasure trove of returned goods, holds potential profits and pitfalls alike. The process of determining what each item is worth requires a keen eye, thorough research, and a bit of intuition.

First, it is essential to meticulously catalog the contents of the pallet. This involves unpacking every item, noting its condition, and identifying any missing parts or damages. The state of an item significantly impacts its resale value. Brand new or like-new items can fetch prices close to their retail value, while items with slight wear or minor defects might need to be sold at a discount. Severely damaged goods, on the other hand, might only be sold for parts or scrap.

Once the inventory is complete, the next step involves researching the current market value of each item. This can be done by checking various online platforms such as eBay, Amazon, and other e-commerce websites where similar items are sold. It is crucial to look at the sold listings rather than the asking prices to get a realistic sense of what buyers are willing to pay.

During this research, pay attention to the item's brand, model, and any unique features that might affect its value. High-demand brands and models tend to retain their value better than lesser-known ones. Additionally, seasonal trends can influence prices. For example, electronics might sell for higher prices during the holiday season, while outdoor equipment might be more valuable in the spring and summer months.

Another important factor is the item's original retail price. Knowing what an item sold for when it was new can provide a baseline for estimating its resale value. However, it is important to adjust this baseline based on the item's condition and market demand. A good rule of thumb is to start with a percentage of the original price and then adjust up or down based on these factors.

It is also beneficial to consider the cost of any necessary repairs or refurbishments. If an item needs fixing, the cost of parts and labor should be factored into the resale value. In some cases, it might be more profitable to sell the item as-is rather than investing in repairs.

Packaging and presentation can also influence resale value. Items sold in their original packaging or with all original accessories tend to fetch higher prices. Therefore, it is worthwhile to keep any packaging materials and ensure that items are presented in the best possible condition.

Additionally, the platform where the item is sold can affect its resale value. Different platforms have varying fees, audience reach, and levels of competition. For instance, selling on Amazon might incur higher fees compared to eBay, but it also provides access to a larger customer base. Weighing these factors can help determine the best platform for maximizing profits.

Finally, it is important to stay updated on market trends and consumer preferences. The resale market is dynamic, and prices can fluctuate based on supply and demand. Keeping an eye on these trends can help in making timely decisions about when to sell certain items for the best possible price.

Estimating the resale value of items in Amazon return pallets is both an art and a science. With careful evaluation, thorough research, and a strategic approach, it is possible to unlock the hidden value within each pallet and turn potential returns into profitable sales.

MAKING INFORMED DECISIONS

At the heart of this process lies the ability to make informed decisions, a skill that differentiates successful ventures from the less fortunate ones. To do so, one must delve into various aspects of the return pallet business, examining each with a critical eye.

Thorough research is the starting point. Understanding the dynamics of the market, including current trends and consumer preferences, lays the foundation for making sound choices. Investigating the types of products that are consistently in demand can significantly impact the profitability of your purchases. For instance, electronics and home goods often maintain high resale value, whereas fashion items may fluctuate more due to seasonal trends.

Assessing the condition of the pallets is paramount. Amazon return pallets come in various states, from nearly new to visibly used or damaged. Scrutinizing the manifest, if available, provides insights into the contents and their potential resale value. Some pallets may contain high-value items that require minimal refurbishment, while others might be laden with goods that need significant repair or may only be sold for parts. Weighing these factors helps in estimating potential profits and understanding the level of effort required for each pallet.

Supplier reputation plays a crucial role in decision-making. Engaging with reputable suppliers who have a track record of transparency and reliability can mitigate risks. Reading reviews, seeking recommendations, and even directly contacting previous buyers can offer valuable insights into the trustworthiness of a supplier. A reliable supplier is more likely to provide accurate manifests and maintain a standard of quality in their pallets.

Cost analysis cannot be overlooked. The initial purchase price of a pallet is just one part of the overall investment. Additional costs include transportation, storage, refurbishment, and marketing. Calculating these expenses in advance provides a clearer picture of the actual financial commitment involved. Comparing these costs against the potential resale value of the items helps in determining the feasibility of the investment.

Diversification is a strategic approach to managing risk. Instead of investing heavily in a single type of product, consider spreading your investments across different categories. This not only spreads the risk but also opens up multiple revenue streams. For example, if electronics sales slow down, profits from home goods or toys might sustain the business.

Understanding your target market is equally important. Identifying who your potential buyers are and what they value can guide your purchasing decisions. Whether selling on online platforms like eBay, local marketplaces, or through a physical storefront, aligning the product offerings with customer preferences enhances the likelihood of successful sales.

Legal considerations should also be part of your decision-making process. Ensuring compliance with local regulations, understanding warranty issues, and being aware of any restrictions related to the resale of certain items protects the business from potential legal pitfalls.

Informed decisions are rooted in a balance of thorough research, critical analysis, and strategic planning. By meticulously evaluating each aspect of the Amazon return pallets business, from market trends and supplier reliability to cost management and legal considerations, one can navigate this complex landscape with confidence. The goal is not just to purchase pallets, but to do so with a clear, strategic vision that maximizes profitability and minimizes risk.

Chapter 5: Purchasing Strategies

BIDDING TACTICS

The excitement of potential treasures hidden within the pallets is palpable, but success often hinges on strategic bidding tactics. Recognizing the nuances of this process can significantly influence the outcome of your investments.

A crucial first step involves thorough research. Before placing a bid, it's imperative to gather as much information as possible about the pallet's contents. Many auction sites provide manifest lists, detailing the items within each pallet. Although these lists might not always be exhaustive or entirely accurate, they offer valuable insights into the potential value of the goods. It's beneficial to cross-reference these manifests with current market prices. This helps in estimating the resale value, ensuring that your bid remains within a profitable range.

Timing plays a pivotal role in the bidding process. Auctions often have peak times when competition is fierce, typically during weekends or evenings. Bidding during off-peak hours can sometimes result in lower competition, allowing for more favorable prices. However, this strategy requires flexibility and attentiveness, as auction end times can vary.

Understanding the psychology of bidding is equally important. Many bidders tend to place their bids early in the auction, driven by the fear of missing out. This can prematurely inflate prices. A more strategic approach involves observing the bidding pattern and placing your bid closer to the auction's end. Known as "sniping," this tactic minimizes the chances of a bidding war, potentially securing the pallet at a lower price.

Setting a budget is an essential discipline in this process. Determine the maximum amount you're willing to spend on a pallet before the auction begins. This prevents emotional bidding, where the excitement of the auction leads to overspending. Sticking to your budget ensures that your investment remains within profitable margins, safeguarding your financial interests.

Another effective tactic is to diversify your bids. Instead of concentrating all your resources on a single pallet, consider placing bids on multiple pallets. This increases the likelihood of winning at least one auction and reduces the risk associated with a single investment. Diversification can also provide a broader range of products, appealing to a wider customer base upon resale.

Building relationships with auction sites and sellers can offer an edge. Regular participation in auctions and maintaining a professional demeanor can sometimes lead to inside tips or early access to high-value pallets. Networking within the community can reveal trends, preferred sellers, and other valuable information that can inform your bidding strategy.

Patience is a virtue in the bidding process. Not every auction will result in a win, and not every pallet will meet your expectations. It's important to remain patient and not rush into bids out of frustration or eagerness. Waiting for the right opportunity ensures that your investments are sound and based on informed decisions.

Lastly, always factor in additional costs such as shipping and handling. These expenses can significantly impact the overall cost of the pallet and should be included in your budget calculations. Being aware of these costs upfront prevents unpleasant surprises and helps in maintaining the profitability of your venture.

Mastering these bidding tactics can transform the experience of buying Amazon return pallets from a gamble into a calculated investment. Each auction is a learning opportunity, refining your approach and enhancing your chances of success in this dynamic marketplace.

NEGOTIATING PRICES

As you delve into the process of securing the best deals, developing a strategy for negotiating prices is paramount. This subchapter will guide you through the nuances of this crucial skill, ensuring you maximize your investment while building strong relationships with suppliers.

When approaching negotiations, preparation is key. Begin by researching the average prices of Amazon return pallets within your chosen category. Understanding market trends and the typical price range will provide a solid foundation for your discussions. This knowledge arms you with the confidence to negotiate effectively, allowing you to discern whether a quoted price is fair or inflated.

Establishing a rapport with suppliers is equally important. Building a relationship based on trust and mutual respect can significantly influence the outcome of your negotiations. Engage in open and honest communication, showing genuine interest in their business and the products they offer. This approach not only fosters goodwill but also positions you as a serious buyer, increasing the likelihood of favorable terms.

When it comes to the actual negotiation, timing plays a critical role. Suppliers often have sales targets and inventory turnover goals, which can work to your advantage. Inquire about any upcoming sales or promotions, and consider negotiating towards the end of the month or quarter when sellers may be more inclined to offer discounts to meet their targets. Additionally, purchasing during off-peak seasons can yield better deals, as demand for return pallets tends to fluctuate throughout the year.

Flexibility is another valuable asset in price negotiations. Be open to adjusting your purchase terms to find a mutually beneficial agreement. For instance, if a supplier is unwilling to lower the price, explore other avenues such as requesting free shipping, additional pallets, or extended payment terms. These concessions can add significant value to your purchase without directly impacting the price.

Effective negotiation also involves strategic communication. Clearly articulate your budget constraints and the value you perceive in the product. Use persuasive language to highlight how a lower price could lead to a long-term business relationship, increased order volumes, or positive reviews. By demonstrating the potential benefits to the supplier, you create a compelling case for them to consider your offer.

Throughout the negotiation process, patience and persistence are vital. Avoid rushing into a decision or accepting the first offer presented. Take your time to evaluate the terms and counter-offers carefully. If negotiations stall, don't hesitate to walk away and explore other options. Sometimes, stepping back can prompt the supplier to reconsider their position and come back with a more attractive offer.

Documenting the agreed-upon terms is essential to avoid misunderstandings. Once a price and conditions are settled, ensure that all details are clearly outlined in a written agreement. This document should include the price, quantity, delivery terms, payment schedule, and any additional concessions made during the negotiation. Having a written record protects both parties and provides a reference point for future transactions.

By mastering the art of negotiating prices, you not only secure the best deals on Amazon return pallets but also establish a foundation for successful and profitable ventures. This skill, combined with thorough research and strategic planning, will set you on the path to becoming a savvy and successful buyer in the competitive world of return pallets.

BULK BUYING

Venturing into the realm of bulk buying Amazon return pallets unveils a world where quantity meets opportunity. The concept of purchasing in bulk, especially in the context of return pallets, can be both tantalizing and daunting. The allure lies in the potential for significant profit margins, while the challenge is in managing the sheer volume of goods and the variability in their conditions.

Imagine standing before towering stacks of pallets, each laden with an assortment of items returned by customers for myriad reasons. The sheer volume can be overwhelming, but it also represents a treasure trove of possibilities. Each pallet is a microcosm of consumer behavior, filled with products that range from brand new and unopened to slightly used or even defective. The key to mastering bulk buying is in understanding how to navigate this spectrum of quality and condition.

One of the primary advantages of bulk buying is the cost savings. By purchasing large quantities of return pallets, you often secure a lower price per unit compared to buying smaller lots. This economy of scale can significantly boost your profit margins, provided you have a solid plan for processing and selling the items. It's a game of numbers, where the more you buy, the better the deal you can negotiate.

However, bulk buying requires a strategic approach. It's not just about acquiring large quantities of goods; it's about ensuring that those goods are worth the investment. This involves meticulous research and due diligence. Start by understanding the source of the return pallets. Reputable liquidators often provide detailed manifests that list the contents of each pallet, including the condition of the items. These manifests are invaluable, allowing you to make informed decisions and assess the potential resale value of the goods.

Storage is another critical consideration. With bulk buying comes the need for ample space to store the pallets until they are processed and sold. This could mean renting additional warehouse space or optimizing your existing storage facilities. Efficient organization is crucial to prevent clutter and ensure that you can access and manage your inventory effectively.

Processing the items in bulk requires a systematic approach. Begin by sorting the goods based on their condition and category. This will help streamline the process of listing them for resale. Items that are new or in excellent condition can be sold at a higher price, while those that are used or defective may need to be discounted or sold for parts. Having a dedicated team or a well-structured workflow can expedite this process and reduce the time it takes to get the items back on the market.

Marketing plays a pivotal role in the success of bulk buying. With a large inventory, it's essential to reach a broad audience. Utilize multiple sales channels, including online marketplaces, social media, and local outlets. Effective marketing strategies, such as targeted ads and promotions, can help attract buyers and move your inventory quickly.

Bulk buying Amazon return pallets is a dynamic and potentially lucrative venture. It requires a blend of shrewd business acumen, logistical planning, and marketing savvy. For those willing to invest the time and resources, the rewards can be substantial, transforming a mountain of returned goods into a profitable enterprise.

PAYMENT METHODS

In the world of buying and selling Amazon return pallets, understanding the available payment methods is essential. These methods not only facilitate smooth transactions but also ensure that both buyers and sellers are protected throughout the process. The most common payment methods include credit and debit cards, PayPal, bank transfers, and sometimes even cryptocurrency.

Credit and debit cards are perhaps the most widely accepted forms of payment. They offer convenience and security, allowing buyers to quickly and efficiently complete their purchases. Most liquidation platforms that sell Amazon return pallets accept major credit cards like Visa, MasterCard, and American Express. Using credit cards can also provide additional layers of protection, such as fraud detection and chargeback options, which can be useful if there are any disputes or issues with the transaction.

PayPal is another popular payment method, known for its ease of use and secure transactions. Many buyers prefer PayPal because it acts as an intermediary, keeping their financial information private and offering protection in case of a dispute. PayPal's buyer protection policy can be particularly reassuring when dealing with higher-value purchases like return pallets. It ensures that if the product does not arrive as described, the buyer may be eligible for a refund.

Bank transfers are also commonly used, especially for larger transactions. This method involves transferring funds directly from the buyer's bank account to the seller's. While bank transfers can take a bit longer to process compared to credit card payments or PayPal, they are often preferred for their lower transaction fees. This method is more prevalent among established businesses and experienced traders who have built a level of trust with their trading partners. However, bank transfers do not offer the same level of buyer protection as credit cards or PayPal, making it crucial for buyers to ensure they are dealing with reputable sellers.

Cryptocurrency is an emerging payment method in the liquidation market, though it is not yet as widely accepted as the traditional methods. Some platforms and sellers have started to accept Bitcoin and other cryptocurrencies due to their decentralized nature and potential for lower transaction fees. Cryptocurrency transactions can be faster and more secure, but they come with their own set of challenges. The volatility of cryptocurrency values can affect the final cost of the purchase, and not all buyers are familiar with how to use digital currencies.

Regardless of the payment method chosen, it is important for buyers to conduct thorough research and ensure they are using a secure platform. Reading reviews, checking the platform's security protocols, and understanding the terms and conditions of the transaction can help mitigate risks. Buyers should also be aware of any additional fees associated with their chosen payment method, as these can add up and affect the overall cost of the pallets.

Sellers, on the other hand, should clearly state their accepted payment methods in their listings to avoid any confusion. They should also be prepared to provide verification of the transaction and maintain open communication with buyers to build trust and ensure a smooth transaction process.

Understanding and choosing the right payment method can significantly impact the buying and selling experience of Amazon return pallets. It is a crucial step that requires careful consideration to ensure both parties are protected and satisfied with the transaction.

Chapter 6: Managing Inventory

ORGANIZING YOUR STOCK

As you venture into the world of buying and selling Amazon return pallets, the initial step to success lies in the meticulous organization of your stock. Picture a room filled with an assortment of items, each with its own story, purpose, and potential value. The first task is to bring order to this chaotic array, transforming it into a well-organized inventory that will streamline your operations and maximize your profits.

Begin by designating a specific area in your workspace for incoming pallets. This area should be spacious enough to accommodate the large boxes and allow for easy movement. Clear, uncluttered space will prevent any accidental damage to the items and provide a safe environment for you to work in. As each pallet arrives, inspect it thoroughly and document its contents. This initial inspection is crucial; it not only familiarizes you with what you have but also helps you identify any high-value items or potential issues right away.

Once the inspection is complete, sort the items into categories. Group similar products together—electronics with electronics, clothing with clothing, and so forth. This categorization will help you keep track of what you have and make it easier to locate specific items when needed. Use clear bins or labeled shelves to store these groups; visibility and accessibility are key. Labeling each section clearly will save you time and effort in the long run, ensuring that you can quickly find and retrieve items.

Consider implementing an inventory management system, whether it's a simple spreadsheet or specialized software. This system should include detailed information about each item, such as its condition, quantity, and estimated resale value. Regularly update your inventory to reflect new additions and sales. Keeping accurate records will not only help you stay organized but also provide valuable data for analyzing your business performance and making informed decisions.

As you sort through the items, pay close attention to their condition. Separate new or like-new items from those that are damaged or require repair. This sorting will help you decide the best sales strategy for each item. New items can often be sold at a higher price, while damaged goods may need to be discounted or sold in bulk. For items that need minor repairs, set aside a dedicated workspace and schedule regular time to fix them. This proactive approach ensures that you maximize the value of every item in your inventory.

Create a system for tracking the movement of your stock. This might include a check-in/check-out process for items that are listed for sale online or moved to a physical store. Consistently tracking your stock will prevent losses and help you maintain an accurate inventory.

Establish a routine for regular inventory checks. Periodically review your stock to ensure that everything is in its proper place and in good condition. This practice will help you stay on top of any issues and keep your inventory in optimal shape. It's also an opportunity to reassess the organization of your space and make any necessary adjustments.

By taking these steps to organize your stock, you lay a solid foundation for a successful business. A well-organized inventory not only makes your day-to-day operations more efficient but also enhances your ability to provide excellent service to your customers.

STORAGE SOLUTIONS

When dealing with Amazon return pallets, one of the most critical aspects to consider is how to effectively store your merchandise. Proper storage solutions are essential for maintaining the quality of the goods, ensuring easy access, and ultimately, maximizing your profits. The choice of storage method depends on the volume and nature of the items you are handling, as well as the space you have available.

For those just starting, a garage or a spare room might suffice. These areas can be easily transformed into functional storage spaces with some basic organization tools. Shelving units are a must-have; they help keep items off the floor and make them easier to sort and access. Clear plastic bins can be incredibly useful for smaller items or those that come without original packaging. Labeling these bins will save you time and headaches when you need to locate specific products quickly.

If you're dealing with larger volumes or bulkier items, a more robust solution is necessary. Renting a storage unit is a viable option for many sellers. Storage facilities offer various unit sizes, allowing you to scale up as your business grows. Climate-controlled units are particularly beneficial if you are storing electronics, clothing, or other items sensitive to temperature and humidity. Security is another critical factor; choose a facility with good lighting, surveillance cameras, and secure access to protect your inventory.

Warehouse space is the next step for those experiencing significant business growth. While this option is more costly, the benefits often outweigh the expenses. Warehouses offer ample space, allowing for better organization and more efficient workflow. Investing in industrial shelving and pallet racks can make a substantial difference in how you manage your inventory. Forklifts and pallet jacks are also worth considering if you are continuously moving heavy loads. Additionally, warehouses often come with the option to customize the space according to your specific needs, which can be a game-changer for operational efficiency.

For sellers with limited space or those looking to streamline operations, third-party logistics (3PL) providers present an attractive alternative. These companies handle storage, packing, and shipping on your behalf. Partnering with a 3PL can free up your time, allowing you to focus on sourcing and selling products. It is crucial to choose a reputable 3PL provider with a proven track record. Look for one that offers real-time inventory tracking, transparent pricing, and excellent customer service. While this option involves additional costs, the convenience and efficiency it provides can significantly enhance your business operations.

Regardless of the storage solution you choose, organization is key. Implementing a systematic approach to inventory management can save you time and money. Digital inventory management systems can streamline this process, offering real-time tracking and easy access to your stock levels. These systems often come with features like barcode scanning and automated reordering, which can prevent stockouts and overstock situations.

Safety is another critical consideration. Ensure that your storage area is well-lit and free from hazards. Heavy items should be stored on lower shelves to prevent accidents. Regularly inspect your storage space for any signs of damage or potential issues. Keeping your area clean and clutter-free will not only make it more efficient but also safer for everyone involved.

In the end, the right storage solution will depend on your unique needs and circumstances. Whether you are just starting with a few items in your garage or managing a large inventory in a warehouse, proper storage is essential for success in the business of buying and selling Amazon return pallets.

INVENTORY TRACKING

Keeping a firm grasp on inventory is crucial when dealing with Amazon return pallets. Effective inventory tracking not only ensures that you know what products you have on hand but also helps in identifying trends, managing storage space, and optimizing sales strategies. The process begins the moment a return pallet arrives at your facility. Each pallet is a treasure trove of potential, filled with a variety of items that need to be meticulously cataloged.

First, it's essential to have a dedicated space for sorting through the returned items. This area should be organized and equipped with all necessary tools, such as barcode scanners, computers, and labeling supplies. As you unpack each pallet, every item needs to be inspected for its condition. Are there any damages? Is it new, used, or refurbished? Such details are vital for accurate record-keeping and future sales strategies.

Once inspected, each item should be logged into an inventory management system. This system could be a sophisticated software solution or a simple spreadsheet, depending on the scale of your operation. The key is consistency and accuracy. Each entry should include essential details like product name, SKU (Stock Keeping Unit), condition, and quantity. Additionally, high-quality photographs of each item can be incredibly useful for online listings and customer inquiries.

Categorizing items is another critical step. Grouping similar products together can streamline the process of locating items when orders come in. For instance, all electronics can be placed in one section, while home goods occupy another. This systematic approach not only makes physical storage more efficient but also simplifies the tracking process within your inventory management system.

Understanding the turnover rate of your inventory is equally important. Some items might sell faster than others, and recognizing these patterns can help in making informed purchasing decisions for future pallets. Regularly updating your inventory records to reflect sales, returns, and new acquisitions ensures that you always have an accurate picture of your stock levels. This practice also helps in avoiding overstocking or understocking, both of which can have financial implications.

Technology can be a significant ally in inventory tracking. Barcode scanners and RFID (Radio-Frequency Identification) tags can automate much of the logging process, reducing human error and saving time. Advanced inventory management software can offer real-time updates, low-stock alerts, and even predictive analytics to forecast demand. Investing in such technology might seem costly initially, but the long-term benefits in efficiency and accuracy can be substantial.

Inventory tracking also extends to understanding the financial aspect. Each item in your inventory represents a potential profit, but also a cost. Keeping track of the acquisition cost, potential selling price, and any associated expenses (like repair or refurbishment) helps in calculating the actual profit margins. This financial insight is crucial for sustaining and growing your business.

Communication plays a vital role, especially if you have a team assisting you. Everyone involved in handling inventory should be on the same page regarding procedures and updates. Regular meetings to discuss inventory status, challenges, and improvements can foster a more cohesive and efficient operation.

Incorporating these practices into your inventory tracking routine might seem daunting initially, but with time, they become second nature. The effort invested in meticulous inventory management pays off by providing a clear, organized, and efficient system that supports the overall success of buying and selling Amazon return pallets.

PREVENTING LOSSES

The world of Amazon return pallets can be an exhilarating venture, filled with opportunities to discover hidden treasures and turn a profit. However, the flip side of this excitement is the potential for losses. To ensure your foray into this arena is as profitable as possible, it is crucial to implement strategies that mitigate risks and prevent losses.

A fundamental step in preventing losses is conducting thorough research before making any purchases. Understanding the various categories of return pallets, such as electronics, home goods, and apparel, can provide valuable insights into the types of products you are likely to encounter. Familiarize yourself with popular brands and their typical resale values. This knowledge will empower you to make informed decisions when selecting pallets, ensuring you invest in items with high resale potential.

Equally important is scrutinizing the reputation of the liquidation companies or platforms from which you are purchasing. Customer reviews and ratings can be telling indicators of a seller's reliability and the quality of their pallets. Avoiding sellers with a history of negative feedback or inconsistent product descriptions can save you from acquiring low-quality or unsellable items. Additionally, some liquidation companies offer manifest lists detailing the contents of each pallet. While these lists may not be exhaustive, they provide a general idea of what to expect, aiding in your decision-making process.

Once you've acquired a pallet, the next step is to meticulously inspect each item. This inspection should involve checking for functionality, completeness, and overall condition. Setting up a dedicated workspace for this task can help streamline the process. For electronics, testing each device is paramount. For apparel, examining for defects or wear and tear is essential. Documenting the condition of each item through photographs and detailed notes can also be beneficial, especially if you need to file claims or disputes later.

Effective inventory management is another critical aspect of preventing losses. Organizing your items systematically—by category, condition, or resale value—can enhance efficiency and reduce the likelihood of misplaced or overlooked goods. Using inventory management software can further optimize this process, allowing you to track items, monitor sales, and manage stock levels with ease.

Pricing your items appropriately is a delicate balance between attracting buyers and maximizing profit. Conducting market research to understand current trends and competitive pricing can inform your pricing strategy. Offering competitive yet profitable prices can increase your sales volume, while setting realistic expectations for potential buyers.

Marketing and presentation play significant roles in preventing losses. High-quality photos and detailed, honest descriptions can significantly enhance the appeal of your listings. Highlighting any unique features or benefits of the items can also attract potential buyers. Leveraging multiple sales channels, such as online marketplaces, social media platforms, and local classifieds, can widen your reach and increase the chances of selling your items quickly.

Lastly, fostering excellent customer service can prevent losses by encouraging repeat business and positive reviews. Promptly addressing customer inquiries, handling returns and refunds gracefully, and ensuring timely shipping can build a strong reputation and customer loyalty. Satisfied customers are more likely to leave positive feedback and recommend your business to others, creating a virtuous cycle of trust and profitability.

By implementing these strategies, you can navigate the world of Amazon return pallets with confidence, minimizing risks and maximizing your potential for success.

Chapter 7: Preparing Items for Resale

CLEANING AND REPAIRING

As you delve into the world of purchasing Amazon return pallets, one of the first and most essential steps is transforming these items from their often less-than-perfect state into something more sellable and valuable. This process begins with cleaning and repairing, a crucial phase that can significantly enhance the resale value of the items you acquire.

When you first open a pallet, the sight can be overwhelming. Items may be scattered, some in pristine condition, others showing signs of use or damage. The key is to approach this task methodically. Begin by sorting through the items, creating separate piles for those that need cleaning, those that require repairs, and those that are ready for resale as they are. This initial organization sets the stage for a more efficient workflow.

Cleaning is the next step, and it's one that requires attention to detail. Whether it's electronics, clothing, or household goods, each category of item will have its own cleaning protocols. For clothing, a thorough wash will often suffice, but for items like electronics or kitchen appliances, more care is needed. Use appropriate cleaning solutions and tools to ensure that each item is restored to its best possible condition without causing any damage. When dealing with electronics, remember to unplug them and, if possible, remove batteries before cleaning to avoid any risk of short-circuiting.

For household items, a gentle but thorough cleaning can make a world of difference. Dishware, for instance, can often be restored to a like-new condition with a good soak and scrub. Furniture may require a bit more effort, such as polishing wood surfaces or using upholstery cleaners to freshen up fabric.

Repairing items is another critical component. This can range from simple fixes, like sewing a loose button on a shirt, to more complex repairs, such as fixing a malfunctioning electronic device. Basic sewing skills can be incredibly useful for mending clothing and textiles. For electronics, having a basic toolkit and some knowledge of common repairs can be invaluable. There are countless online resources and tutorials that can guide you through the repair process for a wide variety of items.

Sometimes, the repairs needed are beyond your skill set. In these cases, it might be worth considering professional help. For example, a watch with a broken mechanism might be best taken to a jeweler, while a high-end electronic device might require a specialist. Weigh the cost of professional repairs against the potential resale value to decide if it's a worthwhile investment.

Throughout this process, keep an eye out for items that might have hidden value. Vintage or rare items can often be worth more than their initial appearance suggests, especially if they can be restored to good condition. Researching these items can provide insights into their potential worth and guide your efforts in cleaning and repairing them.

The ultimate goal of cleaning and repairing is to maximize the resale value of each item. By putting in the effort to present each product in its best possible condition, you not only increase its appeal to buyers but also enhance your reputation as a seller. This attention to detail can set you apart in the competitive market of reselling Amazon return pallets, leading to greater success and profitability in your endeavors.

PACKAGING

Each pallet, a treasure trove of returned items, holds the promise of profit, but its journey from Amazon's warehouse to your doorstep and eventually to your customers is fraught with potential pitfalls. The way you handle packaging can make or break your venture.

Imagine the anticipation of receiving a pallet, each box inside a Pandora's box of possibilities. The first layer of defense is the pallet itself, often wrapped in industrial-strength plastic to keep the boxes secure during transit. This plastic cocoon shields the contents from dust, moisture, and the inevitable jostling that occurs during shipping. But don't let this outer layer lull you into a false sense of security. Beneath the plastic, the true test of your packaging skills awaits.

Once the plastic is peeled away, a myriad of boxes in varying conditions greet you. Some are pristine, while others bear the scars of their previous journey—dented corners, crumpled edges, or even gaping holes. Each box tells a story, and your task is to rewrite it with meticulous care. Start by sorting the boxes based on their condition. Pristine boxes can be left as they are, but damaged ones require immediate attention.

For boxes that need reinforcement, sturdy packing tape is your best friend. Choose a high-quality tape that will withstand the rigors of further handling. Apply it generously to any weak spots, paying special attention to the seams and corners. A well-taped box not only protects its contents but also instills confidence in your buyers, who will appreciate the extra effort taken to ensure their purchase arrives intact.

Next, turn your attention to the contents of each box. Items should be nestled snugly within, surrounded by protective materials like bubble wrap, packing peanuts, or air pillows. These materials act as cushions, absorbing shocks and preventing movement during transit. Delicate items, in particular, benefit from an extra layer of protection. Wrap each piece individually, securing it with tape if necessary, and place it in the box with care.

For electronic items, anti-static bubble wrap is essential. These sensitive devices are vulnerable to static electricity, which can cause irreparable damage. By using anti-static materials, you safeguard these valuable items and enhance their resale value. Additionally, consider using desiccant packs to keep moisture at bay, especially for electronics and other moisture-sensitive goods.

Labeling is another crucial aspect of effective packaging. Clear, accurate labels not only facilitate easy identification but also streamline the reselling process. Each box should be labeled with its contents, condition, and any other pertinent information. This practice not only aids in inventory management but also provides transparency to your buyers, fostering trust and repeat business.

In some cases, repackaging might be necessary. If the original packaging is too damaged or insufficient, transfer the items to a new, sturdy box. Ensure the new box is the right size, with just enough room for protective materials without leaving excessive empty space. Overpacking can lead to increased shipping costs, while underpacking can compromise the safety of the items.

Attention to detail in packaging reflects your commitment to quality and customer satisfaction. By investing time and resources into proper packaging, you not only protect your inventory but also build a reputation for reliability and care. Each box that leaves your hands is a testament to your diligence, paving the way for successful transactions and a thriving business in the world of Amazon return pallets.

PHOTOGRAPHY TIPS

Capturing the perfect image of your Amazon return pallets can make a significant difference in how quickly they sell. When diving into the world of reselling, the power of a well-taken photograph cannot be overstated. Lighting, angles, and clarity all play pivotal roles in presenting your products in the best possible light.

Lighting is the cornerstone of any good photograph. Natural light is often the best option as it provides a soft and flattering illumination. Position your pallet near a large window or even outside to take advantage of daylight. If natural light isn't an option, consider investing in some affordable softbox lights. These can help replicate natural light and eliminate harsh shadows, making your items look more appealing. Ensure the light is evenly distributed across the pallet to highlight every detail.

The angle from which you take your photos can also impact the buyer's perception. Start by capturing a wide shot that includes the entire pallet. This gives potential buyers a clear overview of what they are purchasing. Next, take close-up shots of individual items or sections of the pallet. These detailed images allow buyers to see the condition and quality of the products. Experiment with different angles to find the most flattering perspectives. For instance, shooting slightly from above can often provide a more comprehensive view than a straight-on shot.

Clarity and focus are crucial. A blurry or grainy photo can deter potential buyers. Use a good quality camera or a smartphone with a high-resolution camera. Ensure that your lens is clean and that the camera is steady when taking the shot. A tripod can be a valuable tool to achieve this stability. Additionally, use the camera's autofocus feature to ensure that every image is sharp and clear. If your camera allows, adjust the aperture to create a shallow depth of field, which can make your items stand out against the background.

The background of your photo should be clean and uncluttered. A plain white or neutral-colored backdrop can make your pallet stand out. Avoid busy or distracting backgrounds that can take attention away from the products. If you don't have a professional backdrop, a clean wall or a large sheet can work just as well. The goal is to ensure that the focus remains on the items you are selling.

Presentation is another key aspect. Arrange the items neatly and in an organized manner. This not only makes the pallet look more appealing but also helps potential buyers understand what is included. Group similar items together and ensure that everything is visible. If there are any unique or high-value items, make sure they are prominently displayed. This can entice buyers and highlight the value of the pallet.

Editing can enhance your photos further. Simple adjustments to brightness, contrast, and saturation can make a big difference. Use photo editing software or apps to make these tweaks, but be careful not to overdo it. The aim is to enhance the image while keeping it realistic and true to the actual condition of the items.

Good photography is about more than just taking a picture; it's about creating an image that tells a story and sells a product. By paying attention to lighting, angles, clarity, background, presentation, and editing, you can create compelling photographs that attract buyers and boost your sales.

CREATING LISTINGS

Crafting an effective listing for each item within your Amazon return pallets is both an art and a science. It's a meticulous process that demands attention to detail, a keen understanding of consumer psychology, and a dash of creativity. The goal is to present each product in its best light, ensuring it stands out in a crowded marketplace and attracts potential buyers.

Start with a compelling title. This is the first thing buyers see, and it should be both informative and enticing. Use relevant keywords that buyers are likely to search for, but avoid keyword stuffing. A title like "High-Quality Wireless Earbuds with Noise Cancellation, Bluetooth 5.0, and 20-Hour Battery Life" is both descriptive and keyword-rich, making it more likely to appear in search results.

Next, focus on the product description. This is your opportunity to provide detailed information about the item. Highlight key features and benefits, and explain how the product can solve a problem or improve the buyer's life. Use bullet points for easy readability and ensure you cover aspects like dimensions, materials, and compatibility where relevant. If the item has any defects or signs of wear, be honest about them. Transparency builds trust with potential buyers, and a well-informed customer is more likely to be satisfied with their purchase.

Photographs are crucial. High-quality images can make or break a sale. Invest in a good camera or smartphone with a high-resolution camera, and take multiple photos from different angles. Show the product in use, if possible, to help buyers visualize it in their own lives. Ensure the lighting is adequate and the background is clean and uncluttered. If the product has any flaws, include clear images of these as well. This honesty will prevent misunderstandings and returns, and it can even appeal to buyers looking for a bargain.

Pricing is another critical aspect. Research similar items on Amazon to gauge the market rate. Price your products competitively, but also consider the condition and any unique features your item may have. If the item is refurbished or has minor defects, adjust the price accordingly. Offering promotions or discounts can also attract buyers and help move inventory more quickly.

Shipping details should not be overlooked. Clearly state your shipping policies, including handling times, shipping methods, and any additional costs. If you offer free shipping, make sure this is prominently displayed, as it can be a significant selling point. Efficient and reliable shipping not only satisfies customers but also encourages positive reviews and repeat business.

Customer service is the final piece of the puzzle. Respond promptly to inquiries and be courteous in all communications. Address any issues or concerns quickly and fairly. A positive interaction can lead to glowing reviews, which are invaluable in the Amazon marketplace. Reviews build credibility and can significantly impact your sales.

In essence, creating a successful listing on Amazon requires a blend of strategic thinking and genuine effort to present your products as attractively and honestly as possible. Each element, from the title to the customer service, plays a vital role in drawing the buyer's attention and convincing them to make a purchase.

Chapter 8: Selling Online

CHOOSING THE RIGHT PLATFORMS

Navigating the world of Amazon return pallets can be a thrilling venture, but the first critical step is to identify the right platforms for buying and selling. This process involves a blend of research, intuition, and understanding the nuances of various marketplaces. Each platform comes with its own set of rules, fees, and target audiences, making it essential to choose wisely to maximize profits and minimize risks.

To begin with, online liquidation marketplaces are a popular choice. Websites like Liquidation.com and B-Stock Supply specialize in selling returned merchandise, including Amazon return pallets. These platforms often host auctions where buyers can bid on pallets. The auction format can be advantageous, allowing buyers to potentially acquire goods at lower prices. However, it requires a keen eye and quick decision-making skills to outbid competitors without overpaying.

Another viable option is direct liquidation websites. Companies such as DirectLiquidation.com and BULQ offer a more straightforward purchasing process. They typically list pallets at fixed prices, eliminating the uncertainty of auctions. This can be particularly appealing for newcomers who are still getting acquainted with the market dynamics. Additionally, these platforms often provide detailed manifests, giving buyers a clearer idea of what they are purchasing. This transparency can significantly reduce the risk of ending up with unsellable items.

For those who prefer a more local approach, visiting physical liquidation warehouses can be beneficial. These warehouses often stock Amazon return pallets and allow buyers to inspect the goods before purchasing. This hands-on approach can be invaluable, as it enables buyers to assess the condition and quality of the items directly. Moreover, buying locally can save on shipping costs, which can be substantial given the size and weight of return pallets.

Social media platforms and online forums also offer opportunities to buy and sell Amazon return pallets. Facebook Marketplace and groups dedicated to reselling can be treasure troves of information and deals. These communities often share tips, experiences, and even listings for pallets available for purchase. Engaging with these groups can provide insights into the latest trends and connect buyers with sellers who may not be on mainstream platforms.

It's crucial to consider the fees associated with each platform. Auction sites may charge listing fees, final value fees, and payment processing fees, all of which can eat into profits. Fixed-price marketplaces might have their own set of charges, including subscription fees for premium access or higher visibility. Understanding these costs beforehand helps in making informed decisions and budgeting accurately.

Trustworthiness and reliability of the platform are paramount. Reading reviews, checking ratings, and seeking recommendations from experienced resellers can provide a sense of the platform's reputation. It's advisable to start with smaller purchases to test the waters before committing to larger investments.

Ultimately, the choice of platform depends on individual preferences, risk tolerance, and business goals. Some may prefer the thrill and potential bargains of auctions, while others might lean towards the predictability of fixed-price sites. Local warehouses offer the tangible benefit of inspection, whereas online communities provide a network of support and shared knowledge.

Finding the right platforms is a balance of research, experimentation, and strategic planning. By carefully evaluating the options and aligning them with your business objectives, you can set a solid foundation for your venture in the world of Amazon return pallets.

OPTIMIZING LISTINGS

Crafting an enticing and effective product listing is both an art and a science. It begins with understanding the nuances of the Amazon marketplace and tailoring your approach to meet its unique demands. The goal is to create listings that not only attract potential buyers but also convert those views into sales.

The first step in optimizing your listings is selecting the right keywords. Keywords are the backbone of Amazon's search algorithm. Conduct thorough research to identify the most relevant and high-traffic keywords for your products. Tools like Amazon's own keyword planner, as well as third-party options such as Helium 10 or Jungle Scout, can be incredibly helpful. Integrate these keywords naturally into your product titles, bullet points, and descriptions to improve visibility.

Your product title is the first thing potential buyers see. It should be clear, concise, and informative. Include the brand name, product type, and key features. For instance, instead of a generic title like "Smartphone," opt for something more specific like "Samsung Galaxy S21 Ultra 5G, 256GB, Phantom Black –

Unlocked." This not only grabs attention but also provides essential information at a glance.

High-quality images are crucial. Invest in professional photography to showcase your products from multiple angles. Ensure that the photos are well-lit and high-resolution, allowing customers to zoom in and examine details. Including lifestyle images can also be beneficial, as they help buyers visualize the product in real-world use. For example, if you are selling kitchen appliances, show them in a kitchen setting, being used to prepare a meal.

Bullet points are your opportunity to highlight the key features and benefits of your product. Keep them short and to the point, focusing on what makes your product stand out. Use these bullet points to address common customer concerns and questions. For example, if you are selling a vacuum cleaner, mention its suction power, battery life, and any special features like a HEPA filter.

The product description allows you to delve deeper into the details. This is where you can tell the story of your product, explain its uses, and provide any additional information that might help persuade a buyer. Use a conversational tone, and avoid jargon that might confuse potential customers. Be honest about the product's condition, especially when dealing with return pallets. Transparency builds trust and reduces the likelihood of returns.

Customer reviews and ratings play a significant role in a buyer's decision-making process. Encourage satisfied customers to leave positive reviews. Respond to customer inquiries and feedback promptly and professionally. Address any negative reviews with a solution-oriented approach. This not only improves your product's reputation but also demonstrates your commitment to customer satisfaction.

Pricing is another critical aspect of optimizing your listings. Research your competitors and price your products competitively. Consider using Amazon's automated pricing tools to adjust your prices in real-time based on market conditions. Offering promotions, discounts, or bundling products can also attract more buyers.

Optimizing your listings is an ongoing process. Regularly review your listings and make adjustments based on performance data. Utilize Amazon's analytics tools to track metrics such as conversion rates, page views, and sales. Experiment with different keywords, images, and descriptions to see what resonates best with your audience.

Creating compelling and optimized listings requires attention to detail and a deep understanding of your market. By focusing on these key elements, you can enhance your product's visibility, attract more buyers, and ultimately increase your sales on Amazon.

MANAGING CUSTOMER SERVICE

Understanding the nuances of managing customer service is essential when dealing with Amazon return pallets. The world of reselling these items can be unpredictable, but exceptional customer service can turn potential challenges into opportunities for building a loyal customer base.

First and foremost, clear communication is the cornerstone of effective customer service. When listing items for sale, whether on an online marketplace or through a physical storefront, it is crucial to provide detailed and accurate descriptions. Transparency about the condition of the items, including any defects or imperfections, helps set realistic expectations for buyers. High-quality photographs from multiple angles further enhance the listing, offering potential customers a comprehensive view of what they are purchasing.

Once a sale is made, the next step is to ensure prompt and secure shipping. Invest in reliable packaging materials to protect items during transit, reducing the likelihood of damage. Providing tracking information to customers not only keeps them informed but also builds trust. If any issues arise during shipping, such as delays or lost packages, proactive communication can alleviate frustration and demonstrate a commitment to resolving problems.

Handling returns and refunds is another critical aspect of customer service in this business. Establishing a clear and fair return policy is essential. Make sure the policy is easily accessible and understandable. When a customer requests a return, respond promptly and courteously. Even if the return request is due to the customer's change of mind, treating them with respect and understanding can leave a positive impression and encourage future purchases.

Customer inquiries and complaints are inevitable, but how they are managed can significantly impact the business's reputation. Aim to respond to all questions and concerns within 24 hours. Active listening is key; understanding the customer's issue fully before offering a solution ensures that their needs are met effectively. Personalized responses, rather than generic templates, show that the business values each customer as an individual.

Building a robust feedback system can also enhance customer service. Encourage buyers to leave reviews and ratings, and take the time to read and respond to them. Positive feedback reinforces good practices, while constructive criticism provides valuable insights for improvement. Publicly addressing negative feedback with a commitment to resolving the issue can showcase transparency and dedication to customer satisfaction.

Leveraging technology can streamline many aspects of customer service. Automated systems for order confirmations, shipping notifications, and follow-up emails can save time while keeping customers informed. However, it is important to strike a balance between automation and personal touch. Automated responses should be supplemented with personalized communication when dealing with more complex issues or high-value customers.

Training and empowering staff to handle customer service effectively is equally important. Providing comprehensive training on the products, company policies, and communication skills ensures that every team member can represent the business professionally. Encouraging a customer-centric culture within the team fosters a positive environment where employees are motivated to go above and beyond for customers.

Ultimately, managing customer service in the context of buying and selling Amazon return pallets requires a blend of transparency, efficiency, empathy, and continuous improvement. By prioritizing these elements, businesses can not only resolve issues but also cultivate lasting relationships with their customers, turning them into repeat buyers and advocates for the brand.

HANDLING RETURNS

Navigating the world of Amazon return pallets can be both profitable and challenging, but one of the most critical aspects to master is the handling of returns. Whether you are a seasoned reseller or just starting out, understanding the nuances of returns management can significantly impact your bottom line.

When you receive a pallet of returned items, the first step is to meticulously inspect each item. This initial assessment is crucial because it helps you categorize the items based on their condition. Typically, returns can be classified into several categories: new and unopened, like new, used but functional, and damaged or defective. By sorting items into these categories, you can better determine their resale value and appropriate sales channels.

For items that are new and unopened, the process is relatively straightforward. These items can often be sold at a price close to their original retail value. Ensure that the packaging is intact and the product is in pristine condition. A quick check to verify that all components are present can prevent potential customer dissatisfaction down the line.

Items that fall into the "like new" category often require a bit more attention. These products may have been opened but show no signs of use. In such cases, a thorough cleaning and repackaging can make them appealing to buyers. High-resolution photographs and detailed descriptions highlighting the item's near-new condition can enhance its attractiveness in your listings.

Used but functional items present a different set of challenges. These products have been pre-owned and may show signs of wear and tear. Testing each item to ensure it works as intended is essential. For electronics, this means powering them on and verifying their operational status. For other goods, such as clothing or home decor, inspecting for stains, tears, or other imperfections is vital. Once verified, these items can be sold at a discount relative to their new counterparts. Transparency in your listings about the item's condition can build trust with potential buyers.

Damaged or defective items require a more strategic approach. Assess the extent of the damage and determine if the item can be repaired or if it is only suitable for parts. Sometimes, minor repairs can restore an item's functionality, making it sellable again. However, items beyond repair can still hold value for parts. Listing these items clearly as "for parts" or "not working" and pricing them accordingly can attract buyers who are looking for components.

Effective returns management also involves a robust system for tracking and documenting each item's condition. Keeping detailed records can help you identify patterns in returns, such as frequent issues with specific types of products or brands. This information can guide your future purchasing decisions, steering you towards pallets with higher proportions of new or lightly used items.

Additionally, building a good relationship with your suppliers can provide benefits such as better return policies or the ability to negotiate for higher-quality pallets. Clear communication regarding the types of returns and their conditions can also lead to more accurate expectations and reduce the likelihood of unpleasant surprises.

Incorporating customer feedback into your returns handling process is another valuable practice. Encourage buyers to leave reviews and take note of any recurring complaints or praises. This feedback loop can help you refine your inspection and listing processes, ultimately leading to higher customer satisfaction and increased sales.

Mastering the art of handling returns is a dynamic process that requires attention to detail, strategic planning, and continuous improvement. By methodically inspecting, categorizing, and documenting each item, you can maximize the profitability of your Amazon return pallets while minimizing potential losses.

Chapter 9: Selling Offline

LOCAL MARKETPLACES

Nestled within the vibrant ecosystem of commerce, local marketplaces offer a unique and engaging avenue for buying and selling Amazon return pallets. These bustling hubs of activity, often characterized by their diverse array of vendors and buyers, present an opportunity to tap into a wealth of resources and potential profits.

At the heart of these marketplaces lies a tapestry of human interaction. Vendors, each with their own story and expertise, bring to the table a variety of goods that range from electronics and household items to clothing and toys. It is in these lively gatherings that one can find Amazon return pallets, often at a fraction of their original retail value. The charm of these marketplaces is in their accessibility; they are often located in easily reachable areas, making them convenient for both seasoned resellers and newcomers alike.

The allure of local marketplaces extends beyond the mere transaction of goods. They serve as a melting pot of knowledge and experience, where seasoned resellers share tips and strategies with those just starting out. The atmosphere is one of camaraderie, with a shared goal of maximizing the value of each pallet. This sense of community is invaluable, providing a support network that can help navigate the sometimes complex world of reselling.

One of the key advantages of sourcing Amazon return pallets from local marketplaces is the ability to physically inspect the goods before purchase. Unlike online auctions or distant warehouses, these marketplaces allow for a hands-on approach. Buyers can examine the condition of items, check for any damages, and assess the overall quality of the pallet. This reduces the risk associated with blind purchases and increases the likelihood of finding valuable and sellable items.

Negotiation plays a crucial role in these settings. Prices are often flexible, and the ability to haggle can lead to substantial savings. This dynamic adds a layer of excitement to the process, as skilled negotiators can secure better deals and boost their profit margins. It is not uncommon to see animated discussions and friendly banter as buyers and sellers strive to reach a mutually beneficial agreement.

Local marketplaces also offer the advantage of immediate acquisition. There is no waiting for shipping or dealing with potential delays. Once a deal is struck, the pallet is yours to take home and begin the sorting and selling process. This immediacy is particularly beneficial for those eager to get their reselling business up and running quickly.

Furthermore, these marketplaces often host regular sales events or special promotions, providing additional opportunities to score great deals. Keeping an eye on the local calendar and staying informed about upcoming events can give resellers a competitive edge.

While the prospect of diving into local marketplaces may seem daunting at first, the rewards are well worth the effort. The combination of physical inspection, negotiation opportunities, and the vibrant community makes these marketplaces a prime source for Amazon return pallets. With a bit of savvy and a willingness to engage with the local reselling community, one can uncover hidden treasures and pave the way for a successful reselling venture.

SETTING UP A PHYSICAL STORE

The process of establishing a physical store for selling Amazon return pallets begins with selecting the right location. This decision is crucial; it sets the stage for your success. Imagine a bustling street lined with potential customers, or a quiet neighborhood where word-of-mouth can spread like wildfire. Look for an area with high foot traffic, ample parking, and a demographic that matches your target market. Consider the visibility of the storefront and the convenience it offers to your future customers.

Once the ideal location is pinpointed, the next step is securing the space. This involves negotiating lease terms that are favorable yet sustainable. Pay attention to the specifics of the lease agreement, such as the duration, renewal options, and any potential hidden costs. A well-negotiated lease can save you from future financial strain and provide a stable foundation for your business.

With the lease signed, the transformation of the space begins. Picture an empty shell, gradually taking shape into a welcoming and organized store. Start with a layout plan that maximizes the use of space while ensuring a smooth flow for customers. The arrangement of shelves, racks, and display units should facilitate easy browsing and highlight your best deals. Lighting plays a pivotal role; bright, inviting lights can make a world of difference in how your products are perceived.

Decorate the store with a theme that resonates with your brand. Whether it's a minimalist setup with sleek lines and neutral colors or a vibrant, eclectic mix that catches the eye, the decor should reflect the essence of your business. Signage is another critical aspect. Clear, attractive signs can guide customers through the store, inform them of deals, and create a cohesive look.

Inventory management is the backbone of your physical store. Efficiently organizing the Amazon return pallets is key. Sort the items meticulously, categorizing them based on type, condition, and price range. This not only makes it easier for customers to find what they're looking for but also aids in keeping track of stock levels. Implement a robust inventory system, whether digital or manual, to monitor sales and restock items promptly.

Staffing your store with the right team is essential. Hire individuals who are not just capable but enthusiastic about your business. Train them thoroughly on customer service, product knowledge, and store operations. Their interaction with customers can significantly impact the shopping experience, turning casual visitors into loyal patrons.

Marketing your physical store requires a blend of traditional and modern strategies. Utilize local advertising methods like flyers, posters, and community boards to attract nearby residents. Simultaneously, leverage social media platforms to reach a broader audience. Regular updates, promotions, and customer engagement on these platforms can drive traffic to your store.

Establishing a seamless checkout process is vital. Invest in a reliable point-of-sale system that can handle transactions efficiently and maintain accurate records. Consider offering multiple payment options to cater to diverse customer preferences. A smooth, hassle-free checkout can leave a lasting positive impression.

Safety and security cannot be overlooked. Install surveillance cameras, alarm systems, and adequate lighting to safeguard your store. Ensure that emergency exits are clearly marked and accessible. Regularly review and update your security measures to stay ahead of potential threats.

Creating a physical store for selling Amazon return pallets involves a series of thoughtful steps, each contributing to the overall success of the business. From choosing the perfect location to ensuring a secure and welcoming environment, every detail matters.

NETWORKING AND BUILDING RELATIONSHIPS

One of the most pivotal aspects of succeeding in this endeavor is the art of networking and building relationships. This chapter delves into the nuances of forging connections that can prove to be invaluable assets in your journey.

In the bustling marketplace of Amazon return pallets, relationships are the cornerstone of success. Establishing a rapport with suppliers, fellow resellers, and even customers can open doors to opportunities that might otherwise remain closed. Imagine attending a trade show or an industry conference where the air is thick with the hum of conversations and the exchange of business cards. Each interaction is a potential gateway to a wealth of knowledge and resources. Suppliers, often the gatekeepers to the most coveted return pallets, are more likely to offer you the best deals if they know and trust you. It's not just about making a purchase; it's about cultivating a mutual understanding and respect.

One effective way to build these relationships is through consistent and clear communication. Regularly touching base with your suppliers, whether through emails, phone calls, or face-to-face meetings, helps to keep you on their radar. It's about more than just business transactions; it's about showing genuine interest in their operations and challenges. This approach fosters a sense of partnership rather than a mere buyer-seller dynamic.

Engaging with fellow resellers can also be incredibly beneficial. These are individuals who share your passion and challenges, and they can offer insights that you might not have considered. Online forums, social media groups, and local meetups are excellent platforms to connect with peers. Sharing experiences, tips, and even cautionary tales can help you navigate the complexities of the Amazon return pallet market more effectively. These interactions often lead to collaborations, whether it's pooling resources for a larger purchase or sharing logistics to reduce costs.

Building relationships with customers is equally crucial. A satisfied customer is not just a one-time buyer but a potential repeat client and advocate for your business. Providing exceptional customer service, being transparent about the condition of the items, and addressing any issues promptly can help in building a loyal customer base. Word-of-mouth recommendations and positive reviews are powerful tools in attracting more buyers.

Networking also extends to leveraging technology and social media. Platforms like LinkedIn can be instrumental in connecting with industry professionals and staying updated on market trends. Engaging in discussions, sharing relevant content, and showcasing your expertise can position you as a knowledgeable and trustworthy player in the market.

The foundation of all these relationships is trust. Trust is built over time through consistent actions and integrity. Whether it's honoring your commitments, being transparent in your dealings, or going the extra mile to assist someone, these actions collectively foster trust. This trust becomes your reputation, and in the world of Amazon return pallets, a good reputation is invaluable.

In essence, the realm of Amazon return pallets is not just a marketplace but a community. A community where every relationship, every handshake, and every conversation plays a crucial role in your success. Building and nurturing these relationships requires effort, patience, and sincerity, but the rewards are well worth it. Through these connections, you gain access to better opportunities, invaluable insights, and a supportive network that propels your business forward.

EVENTS AND FAIRS

The bustling atmosphere of events and fairs presents a unique opportunity for both seasoned and novice buyers. These lively gatherings are a treasure trove of information, offering an immersive experience that can significantly enhance your understanding of the industry. Walking into one of these events, you are immediately enveloped by a vibrant tapestry of conversations, demonstrations, and negotiations. The air is thick with the aroma of opportunity, mingling with the scent of freshly unpacked merchandise.

The sheer variety of items on display is astounding. Tables and booths overflow with a kaleidoscope of products, from electronics and home goods to apparel and toys. Each pallet tells a story, a narrative woven from the threads of consumer returns and overstock items. Vendors, with their seasoned eyes, can often discern the hidden gems within these stacks. Engaging with them can offer invaluable insights. Many are willing to share their experiences, recounting tales of unexpected finds and profitable resales.

These events are not just about the products but also about the people. The camaraderie among attendees is palpable. Conversations flow easily, as everyone shares a common interest.

Networking becomes second nature; business cards are exchanged, and new connections are forged. This community spirit is one of the most rewarding aspects, providing a support system and a wealth of collective knowledge. Experienced buyers often become mentors, guiding newcomers through the complexities of the trade.

Workshops and seminars are a staple feature at these fairs. Experts take the stage, offering tips on everything from identifying high-value pallets to effective resale strategies. These sessions are a goldmine of information, often revealing industry secrets that can give you a competitive edge. Taking diligent notes and asking questions can turn these learning opportunities into actionable strategies. The hands-on demonstrations, where professionals unpack pallets in real-time, provide a practical glimpse into the sorting and evaluation process.

Many events also feature auctions, where pallets are sold to the highest bidder. The thrill of the auction floor is unmatched. The rapid-fire bidding, the anticipation, and the strategic plays all contribute to an electrifying experience. Winning a bid is not just about the purchase; it's a testament to your growing expertise and intuition. Observing seasoned bidders can also be highly educational, offering lessons in reading the room and making calculated decisions under pressure.

The logistics of attending these events are worth considering. Preparation is key. Comfortable attire and sturdy shoes are a must, given the extensive walking and standing involved. A notebook or a digital device for recording important information can be incredibly useful. Arriving early ensures you get the first look at the pallets and can secure a good spot for workshops and auctions.

Navigating these events with a clear plan can maximize your experience. Prioritize the booths and sessions you want to visit, but remain flexible enough to explore unexpected opportunities. Engage actively with vendors and fellow buyers; their insights can be as valuable as the products themselves. Stay alert and observe the nuances of transactions and negotiations around you.

Leaving the event, you carry more than just purchased pallets. The knowledge gained, connections made, and experiences shared are the real treasures. These elements form the foundation for a successful venture into the world of Amazon return pallets, equipping you with the tools needed to thrive in this dynamic and ever-evolving marketplace.

Chapter 10: Marketing Your Business

BUILDING A BRAND

Creating a brand is the foundation of any successful business venture, and this is especially true when it comes to buying and selling Amazon return pallets. This subchapter delves into the nuances of establishing a brand that not only stands out but also resonates with your target audience. A well-crafted brand can be the difference between a fleeting interest and a loyal customer base.

The first step in building a brand is identifying your niche. Understanding the specific market segment you want to cater to is crucial. Amazon return pallets encompass a wide variety of products, from electronics to home goods, apparel, and more. Deciding whether to focus on a particular category or offer a diverse range of items will shape your brand's identity. Conducting thorough market research can provide valuable insights into consumer preferences, competition, and potential gaps in the market that your brand can fill.

Once the niche is defined, the next step is to create a compelling brand story. This narrative should communicate the values, mission, and vision of your business. A strong brand story can create an emotional connection with customers, making them more likely to choose your products over competitors. Consider what inspired you to start this venture, the challenges you've overcome, and the unique value you bring to the market. Authenticity is key; customers can easily discern when a brand is genuine versus when it is merely trying to capitalize on trends.

Visual identity is another critical component of brand building. This includes your logo, color scheme, typography, and overall design aesthetic. These elements should be cohesive and reflect the essence of your brand. Investing in professional design services can be worthwhile, as a polished and visually appealing brand can instill confidence in potential customers. Consistency across all platforms—whether it's your website, social media, or packaging—helps in establishing a recognizable and trustworthy brand.

In addition to visual identity, the tone of voice your brand adopts plays a significant role in shaping customer perceptions. Whether you choose a formal, professional tone or a more casual, friendly approach, it should align with your brand's personality and resonate with your target audience. Crafting engaging and informative content, whether through blog posts, social media updates, or product descriptions, can reinforce your brand's voice and provide value to your customers.

Building a strong online presence is indispensable in today's digital age. A user-friendly, well-designed website serves as the cornerstone of your online identity. It should provide detailed information about your products, easy navigation, and a seamless shopping experience. Search engine optimization (SEO) techniques can help increase your website's visibility, driving organic traffic and potential sales.

Social media platforms offer another avenue to connect with your audience and amplify your brand's reach. Regularly posting high-quality content, engaging with followers, and leveraging influencer partnerships can enhance your brand's visibility and credibility. Paid advertising on these platforms can also be a cost-effective way to target specific demographics and drive traffic to your website.

Customer service is an often-overlooked aspect of brand building but is crucial in fostering customer loyalty and positive word-of-mouth. Prompt, courteous, and effective communication can turn a one-time buyer into a repeat customer. Implementing feedback mechanisms, such as surveys or reviews, can provide valuable insights into areas for improvement and demonstrate to customers that their opinions are valued.

Building a brand is an ongoing process that requires dedication, creativity, and strategic planning. By focusing on these key elements—identifying your niche, crafting a compelling brand story, developing a strong visual identity, establishing a consistent tone of voice, building an online presence, and prioritizing customer service—you can create a brand that not only stands out in the crowded market of Amazon return pallets but also fosters lasting customer relationships.

SOCIAL MEDIA STRATEGIES

In the bustling world of e-commerce, leveraging social media platforms can significantly amplify your success in buying and selling Amazon return pallets. Understanding and implementing effective social media strategies is akin to unlocking a treasure trove of potential customers and dedicated followers.

Begin by identifying the social media platforms that align best with your target audience. Facebook, Instagram, Twitter, and Pinterest each offer unique benefits and user demographics. Facebook's vast user base and versatile advertising options make it ideal for reaching a broad audience and engaging in community-building.

Instagram's visual-centric approach is perfect for showcasing the diverse range of products you acquire from return pallets. The platform's Stories and Reels features offer creative ways to highlight daily deals or unboxing videos, fostering a sense of immediacy and excitement. Twitter can be utilized for quick updates, customer interactions, and promoting time-sensitive offers. Pinterest serves as an excellent platform for visually appealing product boards, drawing in users who are often in a purchasing mindset.

Crafting engaging content is the cornerstone of a robust social media strategy. High-quality photos and videos that showcase your products in an appealing light are imperative. Utilize various content types such as unboxing videos, before-and-after transformations, or customer testimonials. These not only build trust but also encourage user interaction and sharing. Consistency in posting schedules helps maintain audience interest and fosters a sense of reliability.

Building a community around your brand is another pivotal aspect. Engage with your audience by responding to comments, messages, and reviews. Host giveaways or contests to incentivize participation and attract new followers. Encouraging user-generated content, where customers share their purchases and experiences, can significantly boost your credibility and reach.

Leveraging hashtags effectively can also increase the visibility of your posts, drawing in users who are searching for specific products or deals.

Paid advertising on social media platforms can further enhance your reach. Facebook Ads Manager offers detailed targeting options, allowing you to hone in on specific demographics, interests, and behaviors. Instagram's advertising options, integrated with Facebook's, provide similar advantages but with a focus on visual appeal. Twitter ads can be used to promote tweets and trends, while Pinterest's promoted pins can drive traffic directly to your product listings.

Collaborating with influencers and bloggers who have a following that aligns with your target market can offer a significant boost. These influencers can provide authentic reviews and endorsements of your products, reaching a wider audience and lending credibility to your brand. Ensure that any collaborations are genuine and align with your brand values to maintain trust with your audience.

Monitoring and analyzing your social media efforts is crucial for ongoing success. Utilize analytics tools provided by each platform to track engagement, reach, and conversion rates. These insights can guide adjustments to your strategy, ensuring that you are continually optimizing your approach to meet your business goals.

By strategically employing social media, you not only increase your visibility but also build a loyal customer base. The dynamic nature of these platforms allows for creative and interactive ways to connect with potential buyers, ultimately driving the success of your Amazon return pallet business.

EMAIL MARKETING

Email marketing stands as a powerful tool in the arsenal of anyone looking to profit from Amazon return pallets. It is a direct line to potential buyers, allowing for personalized communication that can turn casual interest into committed purchases. The essence of email marketing lies in its ability to build relationships, cultivate trust, and drive sales through strategic messaging.

The first step in crafting an effective email marketing strategy is to build a robust email list. This list should be composed of individuals who have shown an interest in your offerings or have made purchases in the past. To grow this list, consider offering incentives such as exclusive discounts, early access to new inventory, or informative content about the benefits of purchasing Amazon return pallets. Opt-in forms on your website, social media campaigns, and collaborations with influencers can also contribute to a growing subscriber base.

Segmenting your email list is crucial for delivering relevant content to your audience. Different segments may include new subscribers, repeat customers, and those who have shown interest but have not yet made a purchase. Tailoring your messages to these distinct groups ensures that your emails resonate with their specific interests and needs. For example, new subscribers might appreciate a welcome series that introduces them to your business and highlights the unique value of Amazon return pallets, while repeat customers might be more interested in loyalty rewards or exclusive offers.

The content of your emails should be engaging, informative, and aligned with your brand's voice. High-quality images of your products, compelling subject lines, and clear calls-to-action can significantly impact your open and click-through rates. Including customer testimonials or case studies can also build credibility and trust. Remember to keep your emails concise and focused, ensuring that the recipient can quickly grasp the key message and take the desired action.

Timing and frequency of your emails play a critical role in maintaining subscriber engagement without overwhelming them. Regular newsletters, limited-time offers, and updates about new inventory arrivals can keep your audience informed and excited. However, it is important to strike a balance; too frequent emails may lead to unsubscribes, while too infrequent emails might result in your audience forgetting about your business. Monitoring open rates, click-through rates, and unsubscribe rates can help you refine your timing and frequency to optimize engagement.

Automation tools can greatly enhance the efficiency and effectiveness of your email marketing efforts. Automated welcome emails, abandoned cart reminders, and post-purchase follow-ups can provide timely and relevant communication without requiring constant manual input. These tools can also help you track and analyze the performance of your campaigns, offering insights into what works best for your audience.

Compliance with email marketing regulations, such as the CAN-SPAM Act, is essential to maintain your reputation and avoid legal issues. Ensure that your emails include a clear way for recipients to opt-out or unsubscribe, and respect their preferences promptly. Transparency in your communications and respect for your subscribers' privacy can foster a positive relationship and encourage long-term loyalty.

In the realm of buying and selling Amazon return pallets, email marketing offers a direct and personalized way to connect with potential buyers. By building a targeted email list, crafting engaging content, and leveraging automation tools, you can create a powerful marketing channel that drives sales and cultivates lasting customer relationships.

ADVERTISING ONLINE AND OFFLINE

In the ever-evolving world of buying and selling Amazon return pallets, mastering the art of advertising both online and offline is crucial to success. Effective advertising not only attracts potential buyers but also builds a reputable brand that can drive long-term business growth. Understanding the nuances of both online and offline advertising will provide a comprehensive strategy that maximizes reach and impact.

Online advertising offers a plethora of platforms and tools that can be leveraged to target a broad or specific audience. Social media platforms like Facebook, Instagram, and Twitter allow sellers to create engaging content that showcases their unique offerings. High-quality photos and videos of the return pallets can highlight the value and potential of the products inside. Utilizing hashtags and engaging with followers through comments and direct messages can create a community of loyal customers who are excited about new arrivals and special deals.

Paid advertising on these platforms can further enhance visibility. Platforms like Facebook Ads and Google AdWords provide targeted advertising options that allow sellers to reach specific demographics based on interests, location, and purchasing behavior. These ads can be tailored to promote special sales, new stock arrivals, or even educational content about the benefits of purchasing return pallets. The key is to create compelling ad copy and visuals that capture attention and drive action.

Another powerful online advertising method is email marketing. Building an email list of interested customers and sending out regular newsletters can keep your audience informed and engaged. These newsletters can include information about upcoming sales, new inventory, and exclusive discounts. Personalizing emails and segmenting the audience based on their buying history can make the communication more relevant and effective.

Search engine optimization (SEO) is another critical aspect of online advertising. Ensuring that your website and online store are optimized for search engines can increase organic traffic. This means using relevant keywords, creating high-quality content, and ensuring a user-friendly experience on your site. Blogging about topics related to Amazon return pallets, such as tips for refurbishing items or success stories from other buyers, can also attract visitors and establish your authority in the niche.

While online advertising is essential, offline methods should not be overlooked. Traditional advertising techniques, such as flyers, posters, and business cards, can be highly effective, especially in local markets. Distributing these materials in strategic locations like community centers, bulletin boards, and local businesses can attract a local customer base. Participating in local events, flea markets, and trade shows can also provide opportunities to showcase your products and network with potential buyers.

Word-of-mouth is another powerful offline advertising tool. Encouraging satisfied customers to share their experiences with friends and family can generate organic referrals. Offering incentives, such as discounts on future purchases, for referrals can further motivate customers to spread the word.

Collaborating with local businesses can also enhance offline advertising efforts. Partnering with complementary businesses, such as shipping companies or local repair shops, can create mutually beneficial relationships. These partnerships can lead to cross-promotional opportunities, where both businesses can advertise each other's services to their respective customer bases.

Balancing online and offline advertising strategies ensures that you can reach a diverse audience and create a strong brand presence. Each method has its unique advantages and, when used together, can create a comprehensive and effective advertising strategy that drives sales and fosters business growth in the world of Amazon return pallets.

Chapter 11: Scaling Your Business

EXPANDING YOUR INVENTORY

Amazon return pallets opens doors to a treasure trove of opportunities, each promising a unique blend of excitement and profitability. The key to unlocking these benefits lies in expanding your inventory strategically, ensuring that each addition to your stockpile serves a purpose and enhances your business's value proposition.

Imagine walking into a vast warehouse, rows of pallets stretching out before you, each one brimming with potential. These pallets are more than just stacks of returned goods; they are the lifeblood of your burgeoning enterprise. To effectively expand your inventory, begin by understanding the nature of the products housed within these pallets. Each item tells a story—some are brand new, others slightly used, and a few may be in need of repair. Your task is to discern the gems from the rubble, curating a collection that appeals to your target market.

Start by conducting thorough research on the types of products that frequently appear in Amazon return pallets. Electronics, home goods, clothing, and toys are common categories, but the specifics can vary widely. Identify niches that align with your business strengths and customer preferences. This targeted approach not only streamlines your purchasing decisions but also maximizes the potential for profit.

Next, consider the condition of the items within the pallets. Some products may be in pristine condition, returned simply because of buyer's remorse or minor shipping issues. These items can be resold at near-retail prices, offering a substantial return on investment. Others might require a bit of TLC—cleaning, minor repairs, or repackaging. Assess your ability to refurbish these goods, as this can significantly increase their resale value. For items that are beyond repair, think creatively about how they might still be of use—perhaps as parts or raw materials for other products.

Building relationships with reliable suppliers is crucial in this endeavor. Trusted suppliers can provide detailed manifests of their pallets, giving you a clearer picture of what you're buying. These manifests are invaluable, offering insights into the types of products, their conditions, and potential resale values. Cultivating these relationships can lead to better deals, exclusive offers, and a consistent supply of high-quality inventory.

Storage and organization are also key components of expanding your inventory effectively. As you acquire more pallets, having a well-organized storage system becomes essential. Invest in shelving, bins, and labeling systems to keep track of your stock. This not only makes it easier to locate items when they sell but also helps in conducting regular inventory checks, ensuring that nothing gets lost or overlooked.

Marketing your expanded inventory is the final piece of the puzzle. Utilize online platforms, social media, and local markets to showcase your diverse range of products. High-quality photos, detailed descriptions, and competitive pricing will attract buyers and drive sales. Consider bundling items together for added value or offering discounts on bulk purchases to move inventory quickly.

Expanding your inventory through Amazon return pallets is a dynamic process, requiring a blend of research, strategic purchasing, and effective marketing. By carefully selecting and managing your stock, you can transform returned goods into a profitable and thriving business.

HIRING HELP

One of the most critical aspects of this business is recognizing when and how to bring in additional help. This step can not only streamline operations but also significantly boost efficiency and profitability.

Identifying the right moment to seek assistance is crucial. Initially, as you dive into the world of Amazon return pallets, you may find yourself handling every aspect of the business. From sourcing pallets and negotiating prices to inspecting items and managing sales, the workload can quickly become overwhelming. Signs that it's time to hire help include missed opportunities, delayed responses to customer inquiries, and a backlog of unsorted inventory. These indicators suggest that additional hands could help maintain the quality and timeliness of your operations.

The first role you might consider filling is that of an assistant or general helper. This individual can handle a variety of tasks, such as organizing and cataloging inventory, assisting with inspections, and even helping with shipping and logistics. When hiring for this position, look for someone who is detail-oriented, reliable, and has a basic understanding of e-commerce. Their ability to manage day-to-day tasks will free up your time to focus on strategic decisions and growth opportunities.

Another pivotal role is that of a sales and marketing specialist. This person can take charge of listing items on various platforms, optimizing product descriptions, and managing advertising campaigns. Effective marketing can significantly increase the visibility of your products, leading to higher sales volumes. A candidate with experience in digital marketing, SEO, and social media management can be invaluable. Their expertise will ensure that your listings are appealing and reach the right audience, ultimately driving more traffic and sales.

For those dealing with a large volume of returns, hiring a dedicated customer service representative can be a game-changer. This person will handle all customer interactions, from answering queries to resolving complaints. Excellent customer service can set you apart from competitors and foster repeat business. Look for someone with strong communication skills, patience, and a knack for problem-solving. Their role will be crucial in maintaining a positive reputation and ensuring customer satisfaction.

In addition to these roles, consider bringing in specialized help as needed. For instance, a logistics coordinator can streamline your shipping processes, ensuring that items are delivered promptly and cost-effectively. An accountant or bookkeeper can manage your finances, keeping track of expenses, revenues, and taxes. These specialized roles can provide the expertise needed to run a smooth and efficient operation.

When hiring, it's essential to conduct thorough interviews and background checks. Look for candidates who not only have the necessary skills but also align with your business values and goals. A trial period can be an effective way to assess their fit and performance before making a long-term commitment.

Onboarding new hires should involve comprehensive training to ensure they understand your processes and standards. Clear communication and regular check-ins will help integrate them into your team and keep everyone aligned. Providing ongoing support and opportunities for professional development can also foster a motivated and loyal workforce.

By strategically hiring help, you can scale your business more effectively, improve operational efficiency, and enhance customer satisfaction. Each new team member brings unique strengths and skills, contributing to the overall success of your Amazon return pallets venture.

AUTOMATING PROCESSES

In the fast-paced world of buying and selling Amazon return pallets, efficiency is not just a luxury; it's a necessity. The sheer volume of goods and the rapid turnover can overwhelm even the most seasoned entrepreneur. Here is where the magic of automation steps in, transforming what can be a labor-intensive business into a streamlined, well-oiled machine.

The first step in automating processes is to identify repetitive tasks that consume valuable time and resources. For instance, sorting and categorizing items from Amazon return pallets can be incredibly time-consuming. Utilizing inventory management software can significantly reduce manual labor. These systems can automatically scan barcodes, categorize items, and update stock levels in real-time. This not only saves hours of work but also minimizes human error, ensuring that your inventory is always accurate and up-to-date.

Shipping and logistics are another area ripe for automation. With the integration of shipping software, the process of generating shipping labels, tracking packages, and managing returns becomes seamless. This software can automatically select the most cost-effective shipping options, print labels in bulk, and provide tracking information to customers without manual intervention.

The result is faster shipping times, reduced costs, and improved customer satisfaction.

Customer relationship management (CRM) systems are invaluable in managing interactions with buyers. Automation in CRM can help in sending personalized emails, tracking customer preferences, and managing follow-ups. For instance, when a customer makes a purchase, an automated system can send a thank-you email, suggest related products, and even offer discounts on future purchases. These automated touches build stronger relationships with customers, fostering loyalty and encouraging repeat business.

Pricing strategies can also benefit immensely from automation. Dynamic pricing tools analyze market trends, competitor prices, and demand fluctuations to adjust prices in real-time. This ensures that your products are competitively priced, maximizing profits while staying attractive to buyers. By automating pricing, you can respond swiftly to market changes without constantly monitoring and adjusting prices manually.

Social media and marketing automation tools are crucial for reaching a broader audience and driving sales. Scheduling posts, managing ads, and analyzing engagement metrics can all be automated. For example, tools like Hootsuite or Buffer allow you to schedule social media posts across multiple platforms, ensuring consistent and timely content delivery. Automated email marketing campaigns can segment your audience and send targeted messages based on their behavior and preferences, increasing the effectiveness of your marketing efforts.

Another essential aspect of automating processes is the integration of artificial intelligence (AI) and machine learning. AI can predict trends, optimize inventory levels, and even assist in customer service through chatbots. These intelligent systems learn from data, improving their accuracy and efficiency over time. Implementing AI can give your business a competitive edge, allowing you to make data-driven decisions and anticipate market needs.

Automating financial processes is also crucial. Accounting software can handle invoicing, manage expenses, and generate financial reports with minimal manual input. This not only ensures accuracy but also provides you with real-time financial insights, helping you make informed business decisions.

Lastly, consider the benefits of automated feedback and review systems. Encouraging customers to leave reviews can be automated through follow-up emails or prompts after a purchase.

Positive reviews enhance your credibility, while constructive feedback provides valuable insights for improvement.

By embracing automation, you can transform the buying and selling of Amazon return pallets into a more efficient, scalable, and profitable venture. Automation frees up time, reduces errors, and allows you to focus on strategic growth, ensuring that your business thrives in a competitive market.

EXPLORING NEW MARKETS

Venturing into new markets can be both an exhilarating and daunting experience for those dealing in Amazon return pallets. The landscape is vast, with opportunities scattered across various niches and geographical locations. To begin with, it's essential to conduct thorough market research to identify potential areas that promise high demand and profitability. This involves analyzing trends, consumer behavior, and the competitive environment.

Understanding local markets is crucial. Different regions have distinct preferences and purchasing habits. For instance, electronics might be in high demand in urban areas, while rural regions could show a stronger preference for household items or agricultural tools. It's beneficial to tailor your inventory based on these specific needs to maximize sales potential. This requires not only a keen eye for detail but also the ability to adapt swiftly to changing market dynamics.

Networking is a powerful tool in uncovering new markets. Establishing connections with local businesses, trade associations, and industry experts can provide invaluable insights and open doors to opportunities that might otherwise remain hidden. Attending trade shows, participating in online forums, and engaging in community events can help build these relationships. These interactions often lead to discovering niche markets that are ripe for exploration.

Leveraging technology is another critical aspect of market expansion. Utilizing data analytics tools can help identify trends and predict future demands. Online platforms and social media channels are excellent resources for reaching new customer bases. By creating targeted marketing campaigns and engaging with potential buyers through these platforms, sellers can efficiently tap into new markets without the need for significant physical presence.

Diversifying the product range is another effective strategy. Offering a variety of items can attract a broader audience and reduce dependency on a single market segment. This approach requires careful planning and inventory management to ensure that the selection remains relevant and appealing to the target audience. It's important to balance the introduction of new products with maintaining the quality and reliability of existing offerings.

Building a strong brand reputation is essential when entering new markets. Trust and credibility play a significant role in attracting and retaining customers. Providing excellent customer service, ensuring timely deliveries, and maintaining transparency in all transactions can help build a positive image. Encouraging customer reviews and testimonials can further enhance credibility and attract new buyers.

Exploring international markets can also present lucrative opportunities. However, this comes with its own set of challenges, such as navigating different regulatory environments, understanding cultural differences, and managing logistics. It's advisable to start with regions that have a similar market structure and gradually expand to more diverse areas. Partnering with local distributors or agents can ease the process and provide on-ground support.

Flexibility and adaptability are key to succeeding in new markets. Being open to feedback, willing to make necessary adjustments, and continuously monitoring market conditions can help in staying ahead of the competition. It's a dynamic process that requires constant learning and evolution.

In the ever-changing world of Amazon return pallets, exploring new markets is an ongoing journey of discovery and adaptation. By combining thorough research, strategic planning, and a customer-centric approach, sellers can unlock new avenues of growth and achieve sustained success in this competitive industry.

Chapter 12: Financial Management

BUDGETING AND FORECASTING

Buying and selling Amazon return pallets requires a keen understanding of financial management, and one of the first steps in this process is establishing a robust budgeting and forecasting strategy. This foundational step ensures that every dollar spent and earned is accounted for, paving the way for a sustainable and profitable venture.

To begin with, it is essential to recognize the initial investment required. Purchasing Amazon return pallets involves an upfront cost that can vary significantly depending on factors such as the size of the pallet, the type of goods included, and the condition of the items. Potential buyers must research and identify trustworthy suppliers who offer quality pallets at competitive prices. Establishing a budget for these purchases helps prevent overspending and ensures that funds are allocated wisely.

Once the initial investment is determined, it is crucial to forecast potential earnings. This involves analyzing market trends and understanding the demand for various products. By examining historical sales data and current market conditions, one can estimate the selling price of the items within the return pallets. This step is particularly important, as it allows for the calculation of potential profits and helps in making informed purchasing decisions.

Another critical aspect of budgeting and forecasting is accounting for additional costs. These may include shipping and handling fees, storage costs, refurbishment or repair expenses, and marketing expenditures. Each of these elements can significantly impact the overall profitability of the venture. By meticulously planning for these costs, one can avoid unexpected financial burdens that could derail the business.

Effective cash flow management is another vital component. Maintaining a positive cash flow ensures that the business can continue to operate smoothly without financial hiccups. This involves tracking all incoming and outgoing funds, ensuring that there is always enough liquidity to cover expenses. Tools such as spreadsheets or specialized accounting software can be invaluable in this regard, providing real-time insights into the financial health of the business.

Setting financial goals is also an integral part of the budgeting and forecasting process. These goals should be realistic and achievable, providing a clear roadmap for the business's growth. Whether it is aiming for a specific profit margin, expanding the inventory, or reaching a particular sales target, having well-defined objectives helps in maintaining focus and measuring success.

Regularly reviewing and adjusting the budget and forecasts is equally important. The market for Amazon return pallets can be dynamic, with prices and demand fluctuating based on various factors. By periodically reassessing the financial plan, one can make necessary adjustments to stay on track and capitalize on new opportunities. This proactive approach ensures that the business remains adaptable and resilient in the face of changing market conditions.

Furthermore, it is beneficial to establish a contingency fund. This reserve can act as a safety net, providing financial support in case of unforeseen challenges or downturns. Having this buffer allows the business to navigate difficult times without compromising its operations or long-term goals.

In summary, a well-structured budgeting and forecasting strategy is essential for anyone looking to buy and sell Amazon return pallets. By carefully planning and managing finances, one can create a solid foundation for a successful and profitable venture. This meticulous approach not only aids in making informed decisions but also ensures the business remains sustainable and adaptable in a competitive market.

MANAGING CASH FLOW

A fundamental aspect of any business venture, especially when dealing with Amazon return pallets, is the meticulous management of cash flow. Cash flow represents the lifeblood of your business, dictating its ability to sustain operations, invest in growth, and ultimately turn a profit. For newcomers and seasoned entrepreneurs alike, understanding and controlling cash flow can mean the difference between a thriving enterprise and a struggling one.

The first step in managing cash flow effectively is to establish a clear and detailed budget. This budget should encompass all potential expenses associated with purchasing return pallets, from the initial cost of the pallets themselves to shipping, storage, and any refurbishment or repackaging costs. By anticipating these expenses, you can better prepare for the financial outlay and avoid unexpected surprises that could derail your operations.

Once a budget is in place, it is crucial to monitor cash inflows and outflows diligently. Keep a close eye on the money coming into your business from sales and compare it to the money going out.

This practice will help you identify patterns, foresee potential shortfalls, and make informed decisions about when to invest in new stock or hold back. Utilizing accounting software can streamline this process, providing real-time insights and helping you stay on top of your financial health.

Maintaining a healthy cash reserve is another vital component of cash flow management. This reserve acts as a financial cushion, allowing you to cover unexpected expenses or take advantage of sudden opportunities without jeopardizing your business's stability. Aim to set aside a portion of your profits regularly, building up a reserve that can support your operations through lean periods or sudden spikes in demand.

Negotiating favorable terms with suppliers and buyers can also significantly impact your cash flow. When purchasing return pallets, seek out suppliers who offer flexible payment terms, such as extended payment periods or discounts for early payment. These terms can provide you with the breathing room needed to sell your inventory and generate revenue before having to pay your suppliers. On the flip side, consider offering incentives to your buyers for prompt payment, which can accelerate your cash inflows and improve your overall financial position.

Regularly reviewing and adjusting your pricing strategy is another key aspect of managing cash flow. Ensure that your prices reflect the true value of the products you're selling, taking into account not only the cost of the pallets but also any additional expenses incurred during the refurbishment and selling process. Periodically reassessing your pricing can help you remain competitive while ensuring that your profit margins are sufficient to sustain your business.

Efficient inventory management is equally important. Overstocking can tie up valuable cash in unsold goods, while understocking can result in missed sales opportunities. Strive to find a balance by analyzing sales data and trends to predict demand accurately. This approach allows you to maintain optimal inventory levels, ensuring that your cash is not unnecessarily tied up in stock that isn't moving.

Lastly, consider seeking advice from financial professionals. Accountants or financial advisors with experience in retail or e-commerce can provide valuable insights and guidance tailored to your specific business needs. Their expertise can help you navigate complex financial landscapes, identify potential pitfalls, and develop strategies to enhance your cash flow management.

By implementing these practices, you can ensure that your business remains financially healthy, capable of weathering challenges, and poised for growth. Managing cash flow effectively is not just about keeping your business afloat; it's about creating a solid foundation for sustained success in the dynamic world of buying and selling Amazon return pallets.

TAX CONSIDERATIONS

Amazon return pallets can be a lucrative endeavor, but it comes with its own set of tax implications that are crucial to understand. Comprehending these considerations can significantly impact your profitability and compliance with legal obligations.

When purchasing Amazon return pallets, the initial cost is just the beginning. This expense is often classified as a business expense, which can potentially be deducted from your taxable income. However, the specific rules around deducting such expenses can vary depending on your business structure. Sole proprietors, LLCs, and corporations each have unique tax regulations that may affect how you report these purchases. It is advisable to consult with a tax professional to ensure you are accurately accounting for these costs.

Sales tax is another critical aspect. Depending on your location, you may be required to pay sales tax on the purchase of return pallets. Additionally, when you resell the items, you are generally required to collect sales tax from your customers. The rates and regulations can differ widely from state to state, and sometimes even within different localities. Keeping meticulous records of all transactions is essential to ensure compliance and to simplify the process of filing sales tax returns.

Income tax ramifications are also a significant consideration. The profits generated from selling items from Amazon return pallets are typically considered taxable income. This means that the difference between your selling price and the cost of goods sold (COGS) is subject to income tax. Accurately calculating your COGS is crucial; it includes not only the purchase price of the pallets but also related expenses such as shipping, storage, and any refurbishments made to the items. Proper documentation and record-keeping are indispensable in this regard.

Depreciation of inventory can also play a role in your tax strategy. Some items in return pallets may depreciate in value over time, especially if they are not sold immediately. Understanding how to account for depreciation can help in reducing your taxable income. The IRS provides guidelines on how to depreciate business assets, and applying these rules correctly can provide significant tax benefits.

Another point to consider is the potential for tax write-offs. Expenses related to your business operations, such as transportation, warehousing, and even certain utilities, may be deductible. Keeping detailed records of these expenses can provide valuable deductions that lower your taxable income. It is important to distinguish between personal and business expenses to avoid any issues with tax authorities.

International buyers and sellers must also be aware of customs duties and import taxes. If you are purchasing Amazon return pallets from another country or selling to international customers, these taxes can add another layer of complexity. Each country has its own set of rules and rates, and failing to comply can result in significant penalties.

Staying informed about tax law changes is essential. Tax regulations can change frequently, and staying compliant requires keeping up-to-date with the latest rules. Subscribing to tax newsletters, attending relevant workshops, or regularly consulting with a tax advisor can help ensure that you are always in the loop.

Understanding tax considerations when dealing with Amazon return pallets is not just about compliance; it is also about optimizing your business's financial health. Properly managing and planning for taxes can help you maximize your profits and avoid costly penalties, ensuring a smoother and more profitable business operation.

FINANCIAL TOOLS AND SOFTWARE

Amazon return pallets requires not only a keen eye for valuable items but also a solid grasp of financial management. Utilizing the right financial tools and software can significantly streamline the process, turning a potentially overwhelming task into a manageable and profitable venture.

To begin with, one of the most essential tools is accounting software. Programs such as QuickBooks or Xero offer intuitive interfaces that help track income, expenses, and inventory. They allow you to categorize each transaction, generate detailed financial reports, and even integrate with other platforms like eBay or Amazon, ensuring that your financial data is accurate and up-to-date. This level of organization is crucial when dealing with the fluctuating nature of return pallets, where the value of goods can vary significantly.

Another indispensable tool is spreadsheet software, like Microsoft Excel or Google Sheets. These programs can be used to create detailed inventory lists, track the cost per item, and calculate potential profits. By maintaining a well-organized spreadsheet, you can quickly assess which items are worth listing and which should be bundled or sold in bulk. Advanced users can take advantage of pivot tables, macros, and other features to automate repetitive tasks, saving valuable time.

Budgeting apps like YNAB (You Need A Budget) or Mint can be extremely helpful in managing cash flow. These applications allow you to set financial goals, monitor spending, and ensure that you are not overextending yourself. Given the initial investment required to purchase return pallets, maintaining a strict budget is essential to avoid financial pitfalls. These apps can send alerts and reminders, helping you stay on track and make informed purchasing decisions.

Inventory management software, such as InventoryLab or SellerCloud, is another critical tool for anyone dealing with Amazon return pallets. These platforms offer features like barcode scanning, automated repricing, and comprehensive reporting, which are invaluable when managing large volumes of inventory. They also provide insights into sales trends and profitability, allowing you to make data-driven decisions about which items to focus on.

For those who prefer an all-in-one solution, platforms like GoDaddy Bookkeeping or FreshBooks combine accounting and inventory management features. These tools simplify the process by offering a centralized location for all financial and inventory data. They also integrate with various online marketplaces, providing a seamless workflow from purchase to sale.

Payment processing tools such as PayPal, Square, or Stripe are also essential. These services facilitate smooth transactions, whether you are buying pallets or selling individual items. They offer security features, fraud protection, and the ability to handle multiple currencies, making them indispensable for online transactions.

Tax software like TurboTax or H&R Block can assist in managing the tax implications of your business. These programs guide you through the process of filing taxes, ensuring that you take advantage of all applicable deductions and credits. Keeping accurate records throughout the year simplifies tax season, reducing stress and potential errors.

Lastly, consider using financial analysis tools like Profit Bandit or Keepa. These tools help evaluate the potential resale value of items in your return pallets. They provide historical price data, sales rank information, and other metrics that can guide your purchasing decisions, ensuring that you invest in pallets with the highest potential return on investment.

Using a combination of these financial tools and software can significantly enhance your ability to profit from Amazon return pallets. By staying organized, making informed decisions, and efficiently managing your finances, you can turn this side hustle into a lucrative business.

Chapter 13: Success Stories and Case Studies

INSPIRATIONAL SUCCESS STORIES

Imagine a small, cluttered garage transformed into a thriving hub of entrepreneurship. This is where Sarah, a single mother of two from Ohio, found her calling. Struggling to make ends meet, she stumbled upon the concept of buying and selling Amazon return pallets. With just $500 in savings, she took a leap of faith.

The first pallet she bought was a mixed lot of electronics and home goods. The contents were a mystery, but Sarah's determination was unwavering. She meticulously sorted through each item, testing and cleaning everything to ensure it was in working order. Her children helped her, turning the process into a family project. They listed the items on various online marketplaces, carefully crafting descriptions and taking photos that highlighted each product's best features.

Within a month, Sarah had sold every item from that first pallet, making a profit of $1,200. Encouraged by her success, she reinvested her earnings into purchasing more pallets. Over time, she developed a keen eye for spotting valuable items and learned the nuances of online marketing. Her garage, once a symbol of her financial struggles, became a testament to her resilience and ingenuity.

Across the country in California, David, a college student burdened by tuition fees, discovered the potential of Amazon return pallets through a YouTube video. Intrigued by the possibilities, he decided to give it a try during his summer break. With a modest investment of $300, he bought his first pallet, which contained a mix of apparel and small electronics.

David's approach was systematic. He researched the best platforms for reselling different types of products and identified the target audience for each item. His background in marketing, though limited, gave him an edge in crafting compelling listings. He also utilized social media to reach a broader audience, creating engaging posts that showcased his products.

By the end of the summer, David had earned enough to cover a significant portion of his tuition fees. His side hustle not only alleviated his financial stress but also provided him with valuable business experience. He continued to buy and sell pallets during the school year, balancing his studies with his newfound passion for entrepreneurship.

In a small town in Texas, Maria, a retired schoolteacher, sought a way to supplement her pension. She discovered Amazon return pallets through a friend and decided to give it a shot. Her first pallet contained a variety of kitchen appliances and gadgets. With her background in home economics, Maria had a knack for identifying high-quality items and understanding their market value.

She set up a small booth at the local flea market, where she displayed her finds. Her friendly demeanor and extensive product knowledge quickly attracted customers. Word spread, and soon she developed a loyal customer base. Maria's modest venture grew steadily, providing her with a sense of purpose and financial security in her retirement years.

These stories illustrate the diverse backgrounds and circumstances of individuals who have found success through buying and selling Amazon return pallets. Each story is a testament to the power of determination, creativity, and the willingness to seize opportunities. Whether driven by necessity, ambition, or a desire for financial independence, these entrepreneurs have turned the challenge of reselling returned goods into a rewarding and profitable endeavor.

LESSONS LEARNED

Amazon return pallets can be both an exhilarating and daunting experience. Each pallet is a mystery, a collection of items that have been sent back by customers for a myriad of reasons. Some returns are brand new, others slightly used, and a few may not function as intended. The experiences gleaned from delving into these pallets offer invaluable lessons that shape a more informed approach to this unique business venture.

Understanding the nature of returns is fundamental. Not every item sent back to Amazon is defective; many are simply unwanted or were incorrectly ordered. Learning to discern the condition of items based on the type of return and the reason given can greatly enhance the ability to predict the value of a pallet. This insight is particularly crucial when bidding on pallets at auction or purchasing them outright from liquidation companies.

The importance of research cannot be overstressed. Before committing to a purchase, it is essential to investigate the seller's reputation and the specifics of the pallet being offered. Experienced buyers often delve into online forums, read reviews, and seek out feedback from others who have previously bought from the same source. This due diligence helps in avoiding potential pitfalls and ensures a more reliable acquisition.

Equally significant is the development of an efficient sorting and testing process. Once a pallet arrives, promptly categorizing and assessing each item is vital. This step involves checking for functionality, determining the item's condition, and deciding the appropriate resale channel. Some items may be best suited for online marketplaces like eBay or Amazon, while others might find a better fit in local markets or through private sales.

One must also cultivate a keen eye for value. This entails not just recognizing high-ticket items but also understanding the cumulative worth of smaller, less glamorous products. Often, the profit margins on bulk sales of lower-value items can be surprisingly substantial. Developing this skill can turn an average pallet into a highly profitable venture.

Networking within the community of return pallet buyers can provide a wealth of shared knowledge and opportunities. Engaging with peers allows for the exchange of tips, strategies, and even leads on particularly lucrative pallets. Building these relationships can also offer emotional support and motivation, especially when faced with the inevitable challenges and setbacks.

Adaptability and flexibility are crucial traits for success in this field. The market for return pallets is constantly evolving, influenced by trends in consumer behavior, changes in retail practices, and fluctuations in supply and demand. Staying informed about these shifts and being willing to adjust strategies accordingly can make the difference between thriving and merely surviving.

Moreover, meticulous record-keeping and financial management are essential components of a sustainable operation. Tracking expenses, sales, and profits enables better decision-making and highlights areas for improvement. This practice not only aids in maintaining profitability but also provides a clear picture of overall business health.

Patience and persistence are virtues that cannot be overlooked. The journey of buying and selling Amazon return pallets is fraught with ups and downs. There will be times when investments do not yield the expected returns, but each experience contributes to a deeper understanding and greater expertise. Over time, this accumulated knowledge transforms challenges into opportunities, paving the way for continued growth and success in this dynamic marketplace.

COMMON MISTAKES TO AVOID

One must tread carefully to avoid common pitfalls that could turn this promising business opportunity into a costly misadventure. It's crucial to be aware of these potential mistakes to ensure a smoother, more profitable experience.

A frequent oversight is not thoroughly researching the supplier. The allure of low prices can be tempting, but without due diligence, one might end up with pallets filled with unsellable items. It's essential to verify the credibility of the supplier. Look for reviews, ratings, and testimonials from other buyers. Engaging with online forums or communities where experienced pallet buyers share their insights can provide valuable information about trustworthy suppliers and those to avoid.

Another common error is underestimating the importance of understanding the condition of the items within the pallets. Amazon return pallets can contain anything from brand-new items to heavily used or damaged goods. Failing to clarify the condition categories—such as new, refurbished, or salvage—can lead to misaligned expectations and financial losses. Always request detailed manifests or descriptions of the pallet contents and condition grades before making a purchase.

Misjudging the market demand for the items in the pallets is a trap many fall into. Before committing to a purchase, conduct thorough market research to gauge the demand for the products you plan to resell. Utilize tools like eBay, Amazon, or other online marketplaces to check the current selling prices and sales velocity of similar items. Ignoring this step can result in an inventory that sits unsold, tying up your capital.

Storage and logistics are often underestimated aspects of this business. Pallets take up considerable space, and improper storage can lead to damage or loss of items. Ensure you have adequate storage space that is clean, organized, and secure. Additionally, factor in the costs and logistics of transporting the pallets from the supplier to your storage facility. Overlooking these logistical details can lead to unexpected expenses and operational headaches.

Pricing strategy is another critical area where mistakes are common. Setting prices too high can deter potential buyers, while pricing too low can erode your profit margins. Striking the right balance requires a sound understanding of your costs, including the purchase price of the pallets, shipping, storage, and any refurbishment expenses. Competitive pricing, informed by market research, can help you achieve a steady turnover and healthy profit margins.

Ignoring customer service is a misstep that can damage your reputation and hinder repeat business. Whether you're selling through online marketplaces or your own e-commerce site, providing excellent customer service is vital. Promptly address customer inquiries, offer clear and honest product descriptions, and handle returns and refunds professionally. Positive customer experiences can lead to glowing reviews and increased sales over time.

Lastly, failing to keep detailed records can lead to financial mismanagement. Track every purchase, sale, expense, and profit meticulously. Use accounting software or spreadsheets to maintain organized records. This practice not only helps in monitoring the health of your business but also simplifies tax reporting and financial planning.

By being mindful of these common mistakes, you can navigate the complexities of buying and selling Amazon return pallets more effectively. Awareness and preparation are key to turning potential pitfalls into opportunities for growth and success in this unique business venture.

FUTURE TRENDS IN RESALE

In the rapidly evolving world of e-commerce, the resale of Amazon return pallets is a niche that is continuously adapting to new trends and technological advancements. These shifts are shaping the future of the industry, presenting both opportunities and challenges for those engaged in the resale business. As consumer behaviors evolve and technology advances, it is crucial to stay ahead of the curve to ensure success in this dynamic marketplace.

One of the most significant trends influencing the future of resale is the increasing reliance on data analytics. Sophisticated algorithms and data analysis tools are being developed to help resellers make more informed decisions. These tools can predict which products are likely to have higher resale values, identify market trends, and optimize pricing strategies. By leveraging data analytics, resellers can reduce the risk associated with purchasing return pallets and increase their profitability.

Another trend is the growing importance of sustainability and ethical consumerism. As awareness of environmental issues rises, more consumers are seeking out sustainable shopping options. This shift is driving demand for refurbished and second-hand goods, making the resale of Amazon return pallets more appealing.

Businesses that prioritize eco-friendly practices, such as minimizing waste and promoting the reuse of products, are likely to resonate with this environmentally conscious audience and gain a competitive edge.

The rise of social media and digital marketing is also shaping the future of resale. Platforms like Instagram, TikTok, and Facebook provide resellers with powerful tools to reach a broader audience and engage with potential customers. Influencer partnerships, targeted ads, and content marketing strategies can significantly boost visibility and sales. By building a strong online presence and leveraging these platforms, resellers can create a loyal customer base and drive growth.

Technology continues to play a pivotal role in transforming the resale landscape. The integration of artificial intelligence (AI) and machine learning into e-commerce platforms is enhancing the efficiency and effectiveness of the resale process. AI-powered chatbots can provide instant customer support, while machine learning algorithms can personalize shopping experiences and recommend products based on individual preferences. These innovations not only improve customer satisfaction but also streamline operations for resellers.

The growth of mobile commerce is another trend that cannot be overlooked. With the increasing use of smartphones for online shopping, resellers must ensure their websites and online stores are mobile-friendly. This involves optimizing site speed, ensuring easy navigation, and providing a seamless checkout experience. Mobile commerce offers convenience for consumers and opens up new avenues for resellers to tap into a broader market.

The expansion of global e-commerce is creating new opportunities for resellers. Cross-border trade is becoming more accessible, allowing resellers to reach international customers. This trend is facilitated by advancements in logistics and shipping, making it easier to manage international orders and returns. By exploring global markets, resellers can diversify their customer base and increase their revenue potential.

As the resale industry continues to grow, collaboration and networking are becoming increasingly important. Online forums, social media groups, and industry conferences provide valuable platforms for resellers to connect, share insights, and learn from each other. Building a strong network can lead to new business opportunities, partnerships, and access to exclusive deals on return pallets.

The future of resale is marked by technological advancements, shifting consumer preferences, and expanding global markets. Staying informed about these trends and adapting to changes will be key to thriving in the competitive landscape of Amazon return pallet resale. As the industry evolves, those who embrace innovation and prioritize sustainability will be well-positioned to capitalize on the opportunities that lie ahead.